One Child at a Time

Making the Most of Your Time with Struggling Readers, K–6

Pat Johnson

Fairfax County Public Schools, Virginia

Stenhouse Publishers
Portland, Maine

Stenhouse Publishers
www.stenhouse.com

Library of Congress Cataloging-in-Publication Data
Johnson, Pat, 1950–
    One child at a time : making the most of your time with struggling readers, K–6 / Pat Johnson.
        p. cm.
    Includes bibliographical references and index.
    ISBN-13: 978-1-57110-434-2
    ISBN-10 1-57110-434-8
    1. Reading—Remedial teaching. 2. Reading (Elementary) I. Title.
LB1050.5.J584 2006
372.43—dc22   2006048526

Cover and interior design by Martha Drury
Cover photography by Katie Keier

Manufactured in the United States of America on acid-free paper
11 10 09 08 07   9 8 7 6 5 4 3 2

For Rick,
the most honest,
intelligent,
humble,
and loving man I know.

CONTENTS

Acknowledgments

1 A Framework for Thinking About Struggling Readers   1

2 Laying the Foundations   13

3 Active Participation   27

4 Fluency   49

5 Self-Monitoring for Comprehension   71

6 Self-Monitoring in All Ways, *Always*   99

7 Specific Support for English Language Learners   127

8 Assessment—Finding Out What Each Struggling Reader Needs   153

9 What Will It Take?   171

Appendix A   *181*
Appendix B   *183*
References   *185*
Index   *191*

ACKNOWLEDGMENTS

Writing a book is probably the last thing I ever thought I would do in my lifetime. "I'm a talker, not a writer," I would tell my friends and colleagues who suggested I should. "I like working with teachers face-to-face, with children in between us." Ultimately, with the continued urging of many friends, teaching buddies, and family members, I took the plunge. Now I can finally thank not only those who gently nudged me to write, but also all of those who have taught me so much over the years.

First, my heartfelt thanks goes to all the children and teachers at two special elementary schools in Fairfax County, Virginia, Garfield and Bailey's. The children in these schools are an absolute joy to work with. The teachers, both past and present, have always made children and literacy their first priority. Thanks to all who worked side by side with me as we tried to support every child in becoming a successful reader and writer. The first- and second-grade teams of Bailey's Elementary, with whom I've spent the last few years, have a special place in my heart.

I'm especially grateful to the terrific group of teachers that I worked with while writing the book—Katie Keier, Carol Felderman, Daisy Bokus, Kara Conques, Stanzi Lowe, and Sarah VanderZanden. They welcomed me into their classrooms, shared their fantastic students, asked incredible questions, and inspired me to continue to learn along with them. Thanks so much for the feedback on my writing, trying out lessons, taking pictures, and conversing for hours about struggling readers and what to do to help them.

To my three recent administrators, Jean Frey, Carol Franz, and Judy Thompson, thanks for creating the kind of environment where teachers are respected and encouraged to grow, and where children feel safe and loved. Every school deserves a literacy leader like you.

A continuous source of professional support has always come from the Language Arts office, Title I department, and the Reading Recovery team of my district. The staff development support they have provided while I have been a reading teacher in Fairfax County Public Schools has been invaluable. I appreciate all they've done for literacy. I would like to thank two very special people, Ann McCallum and Bev Morrison, who were my first mentors. They pointed me in the right direction and supported me in a manner that helped me gain confidence, continue learning, and find ways to help other teachers.

I have much respect and appreciation for all the other teachers I've mentioned in this book, including Noel Naylor, Laura McDonnell, Nancy Kurtz, Carrie Omps, Sabrina Shea, Jodi Maher, Emelie Parker, and Tess Pardini. I thank them for allowing me to tell little pieces of their stories and share how they work with children. I also thank Gina Elliott and Isabel Showkatian for always making space for me in their room and putting up with my odd times of coming and going.

I am grateful to Ruth Powell, teacher of many talents, who read earlier drafts and helped shape my original proposal for the book. It was wonderful to receive feedback from someone who wasn't a literacy teacher. And to Carol Morosco, fellow writer, teacher, and friend—her encouragement and humor kept me going. The enthusiasm and energy for teaching that Margaret Sanchez possesses always kept me running to keep up.

Many thanks to Ann Boley, my Reading Recovery trainer, who taught me so much about the reading process, and to Christie Sens, an amazing teacher, free spirit, and friend, who would get so excited about every small success achieved by each of her students. Both these women were taken from us at too early an age. They are sorely missed.

A very special thank-you and a big hug are reserved for Kathleen Fay. Kathleen planted the original seed in me for writing this book. Though she sometimes calls me her mentor, it is she who constantly nourishes me. Her work in the field of teaching writing, supporting English language learners, and critical literacy has inspired many teachers, including myself. By her gentle manner with children, she has taught me to listen and learn from every single child. I wish every teacher could know Kathleen—my colleague, my friend, and also my niece.

Mary Schulman and Carleen Payne, two extraordinary reading teachers, are both personal and professional role models for me. Our conversations about literacy teaching and learning, and about life, have fueled me in many ways. I thank them for sharing their ideas and knowledge with me, for their input and insights on my writing, for our late-night talks at conferences, and for all the laughs. Carleen and Mary, I'd take a boat ride down the Mississippi with you guys any day!

I'd also like to thank Brenda Power, my editor, who made life so easy as I wrote this book. As a first-time author, I found her guidance and writing expertise invaluable. Also thanks to Philippa Stratton, Jay Kilburn, Tom Seavey, Erin Whitehead, Martha Drury, Doug Kolmar, and all the other members of the Stenhouse family who helped bring this book to completion.

I am so lucky to be part of a very large, but extremely special, extended family. All my sisters and my brother and their spouses and all their collective children have always cheered me on no matter what the endeavor. Thanks to Barb and Jim for taking me in and giving me a home those many years ago when I was just getting started in my teaching career in Virginia.

Of course, a writer always saves the best for last. I thank my husband and daughters for loving me unconditionally as I love them. My two grown daughters, Heather and Jodie, whether living near or far, would always call and offer support and encouragement on my writing. They have brought much happiness into my life and have taught me that being a mom is by far the most rewarding job in the world. And an extra thank-you goes to Heather and my son-in-law, Andrew, for their technical know-how when I had computer glitches.

A final, but huge, thank-you is for my husband, Rick, who never wavered in his attention to me, never complained about eating alone when I was off "in literacy land," never gave up when given the tedious bibliography task, never doubted that I would complete this project, and always, always was there whenever I needed him most. Rick, you have made my whole life richer in so many ways. Thanks for being my husband, best friend, and personal poet.

CHAPTER 1

A Framework *for* Thinking About Struggling Readers

When I suggest that we need to "teach with a sense of urgency" I'm not talking about teaching prompted by anxiety but rather about making every moment in the classroom count, about ensuring that our instruction engages students and moves them ahead, about using daily evaluation and reflection to make wise teaching decisions. Complacency will not get our students where they need to be.

Regie Routman, *Reading Essentials*

Throughout my twenty-five years of being a reading teacher, I've tried to help teachers learn about all facets of literacy—from children's literature and reading aloud well to developing writing workshops and holding successful writing conferences. But in the last ten years I have become more and more fascinated with the goal of trying to understand how best to support the children for whom reading doesn't come easily. And that research has led me to discover ways to help classroom teachers with their children who struggle.

Most classroom teachers are confronted yearly with the task of teaching some of the hardest-to-teach children to read. Though there are intervention programs in place in many school districts that provide extra support for these children (Title I, learning disability teachers, Reading Recovery teachers), the ultimate responsibility for teaching these children to read inevitably falls on the classroom teachers. I want to help the classroom teacher as much as possible to make the most of her teaching time with a reader who struggles.

For many years now, I have heard the cry of these teachers asking for more knowledge, ideas, and teaching techniques.

"I already have a strong reading and writing workshop established in my classroom, but I still have a few students whom I just don't know how to help."

"A few of my students seem to level off or make little progress. These readers need so much help from me; I don't even know where to begin."

"My struggling readers sound okay, but don't comprehend what they read. I've tried everything I know. What else is there?"

In this book we get right down to the nitty-gritty business of sitting next to a child who is struggling in order to:

1. figure out what is blocking the child's progress at this time,
2. teach that particular strategy or behavior to the child, then
3. slowly back off with supports, enabling the child to take on the strategy for himself.

In the opening quote, Regie Routman stresses the need for making the best use of our time every moment of every teaching day. Nowhere is this more applicable than with struggling readers. Teachers who are requesting help realize that, when it comes to readers who struggle, the more tailored the instruction is toward each child's specific needs, the more beneficial the interaction will be for that student. They want to make the most of every encounter with the struggling reader, whether working one-on-one or in a small group.

As I think about teaching with a sense of urgency as Routman suggests, I am reminded of an interaction I had with a principal and friend, Judy Thompson, with whom I worked several years ago. Judy always supported my literacy endeavors in the building; she found funds for more books for the classrooms whenever I asked; she joined the teachers-as-readers groups reading professional literature; and she supported the staff development I suggested to ensure that all our students became proficient readers. One day, shortly before school was to begin, I was rambling on about all that needed to be done in the area of staff development, and Judy said, "Oh, Pat, you just want everyone to be a reading teacher!" I knew she was trying to rein me in from setting my expectations so high for every classroom teacher that they would become overwhelmed. Instead, I answered, "Yes, that's exactly what I want!" I *do* believe that every elementary school teacher is a teacher of reading and needs a certain amount of knowledge about reading process in order to successfully teach struggling readers.

I think teachers want more expertise in addressing struggling reader issues and to feel a sense of accomplishment as well. I once had a learning disabilities teacher confide in me, "I don't have the background in reading that I should to teach these kids. I had one or two reading classes in my college and graduate programs and I've got the kids with the most reading problems!" She was right. An average amount of basic reading knowledge might suffice for many children, but for children who struggle, more expertise is necessary. Classroom teachers and others are ready and willing to expand their knowledge in this area.

Every teacher I have ever worked with has always tried to teach struggling readers to the best of her knowledge. Now they are asking for more information about those few children who stump them every year, those children who cause them hours of sleepless nights. Teachers do not need more tests to tell them *who* is struggling; they already know that. Rather, they want help with how to make their teaching more effective for struggling readers. This book can start them on that learning journey.

Who Is a Struggling Reader?

I have always felt compassion for the teachers in the olden days, teaching in a one-room schoolhouse with all those different-aged children and their varying needs, a lack of supplies, and a scarcity of books. And on top of it all, they had to mop the floor at the end of the day! I ask myself, "How many of us would have survived those conditions?" And while we've certainly come a long way in changing the look of public schooling, the range of children's reading abilities in any one given class today never ceases to amaze me. You can just as easily hear a sixth-grade teacher or a second-grade teacher say, "I have children whose levels range from kindergarten to high school in my class." No matter what the range is in your particular classroom, I can guarantee that you will have struggling readers.

What does the term *struggling reader* mean? Why do these children struggle? And how do we teach them? These are three questions I focus on answering in this book.

Randy and Katherine Bomer write that the term *struggling reader* is misleading because it suggests all struggling readers fit into one category. Common sense tells us this can't possibly be true. The Bomers say struggling readers are "People who, for one reason or another, misapprehended the reading process and have not put a reading system together that adds up to meaning" (2001, p. 89). It is this reading process system, and how children put it together, that all teachers—classroom teachers, reading specialists, learning disability experts, and teachers of second language learners—need to understand well. As Marie Clay (1991) notes, we cannot put the reading process into the head of a child; the child must be the one to assemble the working systems.

In order to better support the children who struggle, a teacher needs to understand the network of strategies that goes on in the head of a proficient reader. How can we possibly help a child who is having trouble acquiring strategies and assembling working systems to solve words and understand text if we have no idea what a proficient reader actually does as he reads? This network of strategies as we understand it today is explained in Chapter 2.

There are many reasons why a child might have become a struggling reader, including lack of opportunity to learn, ineffective early instruction, or emotional trauma during preschool years causing the child not to attend to literacy learning. And there are many more ways in which that struggle takes shape. Some of those struggles can be seen in children who:

- neglect to self-monitor as they read; who read on whether they are making sense or not;
- sit and wait for someone to tell them a word rather than making attempts at figuring it out;
- read word by word;
- rely too heavily on one source of information as opposed to using a balance of meaning, structural information, and the letters and sounds;
- struggle with the reading process in addition to learning English;
- invent text or make random guesses at unknown words;
- call the words accurately but don't comprehend what they read;
- ignore punctuation cues.

If there are multiple reasons why children struggle and just as many ways in which the struggle manifests itself, there is certainly no *one* answer for helping them. In her book *By Different Paths to Common Outcomes*, Marie Clay says, "Multiple causation makes it highly unlikely that a prescribed sequence of instruction would suit all children with low literacy achievement" (1998, p. 225). Allington and McGill-Franzen (1995) have been telling us for years that there is no one "quick fix." A teacher needs to take a careful look at each struggling reader to see what that child does as she reads, juxtapose that information against what a proficient reader does, and make teaching decisions using that information. Observation and assessment of the student while engaged in reading always informs our instruction, and knowledge of reading process guides our way.

A Framework for Teaching Struggling Readers

One successful way I have found to help classroom teachers is to provide a framework that enables them to observe, analyze, plan, and take action toward helping children who struggle. This framework, explained here, follows four steps: (1) here's what; (2) so what; (3) now what; and (4) then what. Stories of teacher/student interactions illustrate its use as teachers learn to guide their thinking about instruction for struggling readers.

It was in the book *Pathways to Understandings: Patterns and Practices in the Learner-Focused Classroom* (1998) that I first saw the technique "here's what/so what/now what." The authors, Laura Lipton and Bruce Wellman, suggest ways to use this general format for school or team planning, for assessing students' knowledge about a new topic, or as a graphic organizer for students themselves to use. On another occasion, a presenter, working with a group of reading teachers, used the format to help us take a careful look at a child in order to make sound instructional decisions. For my purposes, I've added the fourth step, *then what*, which is necessary to confirm the student's assimilation of the strategy or behavior.

Framework Steps

Here's What

This is the investigative stage; a time to find out as much as I can about how a child approaches a text and particularly what the child does when he comes to some difficulty. I observe with an eye and an ear for strategies. I don't just look for what the child reads correctly or incorrectly in the text, but rather I'm searching for what the child *can do, can almost do,* or *cannot do* as a reader.

All of this requires an awareness of the strategies and strategic behaviors that proficient readers use widely. Armed with this knowledge, teachers can discover answers to the following questions:

♦ Does the child ever *predict* a word using meaning? Meaning can come from the pictures, the story or sentence context, or background knowledge. When predicting a word with meaning the child substitutes a word that makes sense for an unknown word. Children can also substitute words that look similar to the unknown word, but aren't meaningful. Lack of any predictions should be noted as well as when the child substitutes a word that makes no sense and keeps on reading.

♦ Does the child *search* for information when stuck on a word? Searching behaviors can take many forms. A child may reread a sentence or part of a sentence; he may search the letters in the word, sounding individual letters or parts of the word; you may notice him searching a picture; or he may search past the unknown word by finishing the sentence and coming back. Children can even search using their background knowledge.

♦ Is the child *self-monitoring* while she reads? Self-monitoring means the reader keeps a constant check on herself to see if she is making sense and if she understands what she is reading. A child who self-monitors stops when meaning breaks down. Self-monitoring for early readers can also mean checking for one-to-one matching, or noticing and detecting when something doesn't look right or sound right. Being able to self-monitor doesn't necessarily mean that the child will be able to fix the error; she's just aware that something is not quite right.

♦ Is the child *active or passive* at the point of difficulty? Does the child wait for someone to tell him the word or appeal to the teacher for help? Or does he make some sort of word-solving attempt? When reading passages without understanding, does the child go back and try any strategies to fix up his confusion?

♦ Is the child *flexible* when attacking new words? Does the child make multiple attempts; that is, if one thing doesn't work, does she try another and then another? Is she persistent? Does she always attempt unknown words in the same way or is she flexible when going about that task?

- Does the child *cross-check?* Is there some evidence that the child is using a balance of sources of information—meaning, structure, and visual information—to figure out words or fix errors?

- How is the child's *fluency?* Does the child read word by word? Or does he put groups of words together into meaningful phrases? Is he using the punctuation to help him decide how the text should sound? Are there sections of smooth reading? Does he slow down to solve a problem, but then quickly pick up the pace after the problem is solved?

- Does the child try ways to *fix his comprehension* when meaning breaks down? Does he go back and reread, paraphrasing after shorter sections of text? Can he make mental images of what's happening in the story? Does he know how to infer and find evidence in the text for his conclusions? Does he ask questions as a way to help himself stay engaged with the text?

If the answers to these questions were all positive we would have a proficient reader with a stable system of strategies in place. Of course, with struggling readers this is not the case. Many of the strategies and behaviors are often missing, and we need to know to what extent. It is important to discover partially correct answers or intermittent use of a strategy. Even if the child does something only once, it is useful to note because it will give the teacher something to build on in the teaching phase.

Teachers can use a variety of methods to observe a student's reading during the *here's what* stage—running records, anecdotal notes, miscue analysis, reading conferences, and checklists. Any of these can give us the answers to the questions listed. *For readers who are struggling, such depth of observation is absolutely necessary.* Remember, these are the hardest-to-teach children and it takes more than a cursory look to figure out what might be blocking the child's progress. With time and experience, any teacher can become an astute observer of children's strategy use.

So What

I often ask myself the question, "So what does this all mean?" as I reflect on what I've discovered about a child who just read with me. It is a way for me to fit what this child is doing, almost doing, and not doing into the whole picture of what a proficient reader does.

As I examine my data, I am looking first for what the child *can do.* I want to know what she has control over, without my assistance. For example, you might infer that a child is reading for meaning because every time she substitutes a word for an unknown word it is always one that makes sense. Knowing what the child can do will give me things to praise. Whenever possible we want to point out and reinforce the strategies and behaviors that the child is using well.

Next, I want to look for what the child *can almost do;* the strategies and behaviors he seems to have partial control over. For example, on several running records, you might notice that the child initiated the first-letter sound 50 percent of the time he attempted an unknown word, whether or not he was able to solve that word. It's important to have as accurate a picture of the child as we can get. I use these partial attempts, where the child did try a strategy, to help him in other places where he did not. What the child can almost do will need to be supported further in the teaching phase.

As I continue to reflect on a student, I am also noticing what she *can't do*. For example, in surveying your assessments you may find that there is no evidence anywhere that the child rereads at the point of difficulty. The strategies and behaviors that the child cannot do will need to be explicitly demonstrated in the *now what* teaching phase.

Prioritizing my discoveries is also part of this reflective stage. I may have discovered four or five different things that I know I could teach this child, but I need to decide what will help him the most at this moment in time. I keep the student's level and the types of books that are appropriate for him in mind as I make this decision.

Spending time analyzing the data and reflecting on a student is all part of planning for instruction. Without this reflection, I tend to be random in my decisions, pulling ideas of what to teach out of the air or off a list rather than having a focus specific to this unique child. *I need to be very clear about what a struggling reader needs.* It's important that I make the most out of every single teaching encounter with this child.

Now What

Now it's time to teach—to actually work with the child getting a strategy or behavior under way. When teaching, I consider the following five actions:

Modeling—clearly demonstrating what you want the child to do, using explicit language
Scaffolding—supporting the child; doing it with him
Prompting—saying something that will remind the child to try the strategy or behavior

Backing off—letting your supports fade away, dismantling your scaffolds, so that the child takes more responsibility for initiating the strategy or behavior

Reinforcing—naming the strategy or behavior that the child used, praising it, and showing him how it worked in this instance.

When I sit with a child, I find myself weaving up and down the whole range of these teaching actions. I respond to the child in a way that fits that particular moment. If the strategy or behavior I am teaching is something that I've determined the child *cannot do,* then a clear demonstration is definitely needed. If I am working on something that the child *can almost do,* then more of my teaching will be in the scaffolding or prompting range. I also remember to reinforce those things the child *can do.* This type of responsive teaching, reacting to the child and what she specifically needs, can be learned by all teachers. You don't have to be a reading specialist to learn how to respond to a struggling reader in this way.

Such responsive teaching is another way of explaining "explicit modeling and gradual release of responsibility" (Pearson and Gallagher 1983), or what most experts define as "best practice" teaching. Most professional books on the teaching of literacy offer some way to make this point. Figure 1–1 shows several of those ways, found in recently published texts. Though each author uses different words, they all mean basically the same thing. Explicit modeling and gradual release of responsibility can be applied to whole-class lessons, small-group teaching, or individual interactions.

Figure 1–1
Explicit Modeling and Gradual Release of Responsibility

Linda Dorn and Carla Soffos (2001)	Modeling	Coaching	Scaffolding	Fading	
Irene Fountas and Gay Su Pinnell (2001)	Show	Support	Prompt	Reinforce	Observe
Debbie Miller (2002) (after Fielding and Pearson 1994)	Modeling	Guided Practice	Independent Practice	Application	
Regie Routman (2003)	Demonstration	Shared Demonstration	Guided Practice	Independent Practice	
Jeffrey Wilhelm et al. (2001)	I do, you watch	I do, you help	You do, I help	You do, I watch	
Pat Johnson (2006)	Modeling	Scaffolding	Prompting	Backing off	Reinforcing

The focus of my teaching when working with a struggling reader can be any one of the strategies or behaviors that proficient readers use. These will be explained further in subsequent chapters. Strategies are the in-the-head thinking that a reader does, such as predicting, self-monitoring, or searching for information. Behaviors are the things we can see or hear the child doing, like rereading, substituting a word, or sounding part of the word.

For some teachers, this type of teaching requires a shift in their paradigm. Teachers who are used to teaching readers mainly about letters, sounds, and sight vocabulary might find the kind of teaching I am presenting to be very different and perhaps difficult. Therefore, I have included very clear examples of what teaching for strategic activity looks like. This book will take you into classrooms for a peek at actual teacher interactions with struggling readers.

Then What

The last stage of the framework is observational. After teaching a child how to use a strategy or behavior, I need to check to see if the child has fully taken it on and uses it independently. Teaching does not automatically guarantee learning. The *then what* stage is a time to watch the child in order to see if the learning has actually happened. "The true test of learning takes place when a student applies the knowledge, skills, and strategies gained from teacher-assisted lessons to independent work" (Dorn and Soffos 2001, p. 9).

It is important not to let go of our teaching focus and emphasis too quickly. Even though a child may be able to perform the strategy without assistance it does not mean that the strategy is fully developed or "fossilized" (Tharp and Gallimore 1988). The child may be using his own self-talk to initiate the strategy or behavior. To become fossilized, the child needs to do the task or implement the strategy automatically, almost without thinking.

My observations in the *then what* phase might be running records or other note-taking systems used while listening to a child read. There may be times when I feel the learning is not as secure as I'd like. I might return to the same focus and demonstrate again. Sometimes I will have to do this in a different way or I may have to spend a longer time modeling before turning responsibility over to the child. Tharp and Gallimore, in their book *Rousing Minds to Life,* say, "The readiness of a teacher to repeat some earlier lessons is one mark of excellent teaching" (1988, p. 39). Struggling readers deserve teachers who are willing to do this.

The observing I am doing in this part of the framework is twofold. I am not only watching and listening to see if the strategy has been independently taken on by the student, but I am also noticing *what else* this child needs. This last phase cycles quite naturally back to the beginning of the framework.

Using the Framework with Teachers

My job as a reading resource teacher allows me to work with teachers, using the framework to help us learn how best to support struggling readers. I learn as much from them as they learn from me. They sometimes see things that I do not because they have the child all day long and know the child better than I do. Our conversations help us construct deeper understandings of struggling readers.

We continually broaden and refine our understandings about reading process, about assessment matching instruction, and about teaching for strategies. What we discover from each new child we work with and each new problem we address adds layers to our knowledge base. Finding the time to meet with another teacher is never easy, but the teachers I work with value it enough that we make our conversations about students a priority. We see how much this careful observation, explicit teaching, and responsive action are helping struggling readers. Some teachers have said:

"I feel like my teaching is more concentrated now. I'm not just doing the next book or level. I'm matching more to what this child specifically needs."

"I'm helping Anna add to her toolbox of strategies. I'm giving her options—and she'll be a better reader for it."

"I've always heard the words *be explicit* before, but now I'm learning what being explicit really means!"

We consider ourselves lucky to have the support of an administrator, Jean Frey, principal of Bailey's Elementary, who provides time and space for this type of collaborative work to happen. In many other schools, classroom teachers have no opportunity to collaborate with a reading specialist or literacy coach about a struggling reader who troubles them. My hope is that the framework and the examples presented in this book will bring those teachers a little closer to the experience of having a coach, and provide them with guidelines for figuring out the best instructional decisions for each student.

CHAPTER 2

Laying
the Foundations

In titling this book *One Child at a Time*, I risked putting off many readers who might think, "That's not for me—I've got twenty-five or thirty kids!" But I wanted to emphasize my belief that each individual struggling reader needs a teacher who is willing to look at that child's unique difficulties. I trust teachers to find their own ways of working with the struggling readers in their classrooms. By examining the needs of even one struggling child with the observational techniques and teaching ideas presented in the framework, you will increase your understanding of reading process and improve ways to teach all the children in your room.

It's important to set the framework of *here's what/ so what/ now what/ then what* within the larger picture of daily classroom reading programs. In this way, teachers can see the techniques and ideas presented not in addition to but as a part of the already-established structures in their regular classroom. It is also important to lay the foundations for the literacy language I'll be using in this book, such as sources of information, network of strategies, and levels of texts. This chapter, therefore, includes basic information on several topics:

- Sources of information that readers use to solve words
- A network of strategies that make up the reading process for a proficient reader
- A balanced or comprehensive literacy environment
- A chart for leveling texts in order to match children appropriately with books for instructional purposes

All these topics are thoroughly addressed in other texts. My purpose here is to present a concise explanation of each. Following each part you'll see a section citing pages or chapters in other references where you can find out more.

Sources of Information

One of the biggest misconceptions that the general public has about the teaching of reading is that when children are stuck on a word they should *sound it out.* Although sounding out will sometimes result in getting the word, the letters and sounds are not the only source of information available to the reader. Since English is not a totally phonetic language (only around 60 percent of our words are written phonetically), relying only on the letters and sounds can often be ineffective in solving the word. Depending on the visual graphophonic information alone to decode words is devoid of meaning. In reality, when readers read continuous text, they draw upon at least three sources of information—the meaning, the language structure, and the visual cues:

1. The meaning of the passage—any available pictures, the student's background knowledge, and the context of the story or sentence
2. The structural information—the student's knowledge of spoken language, anticipating what would grammatically sound right
3. The visual information—the look and sound of the letters, the graphophonics, thinking of other words that might have that letter or cluster of letters

As competent adult readers, we don't even realize how incredibly quickly we use all three of these sources. Let's try an example using a blank to act as an unknown word for us:

She was _____ in the hammock.

There are any number of words that would work here—*lying, swinging, rocking, reading, sleeping, dozing, napping, happy, comfortable,* or even *knitting.* You used meaningful information (many of the things you know a person could do in a hammock) and structural information (notice that verbs and adjectives work here, but not nouns) to put in a possible word.

Now suppose you had more information:

> Jill's eyes were closed.
> She was _____ in the hammock.

You'd have to narrow down your choices. Because you took in further meaningful information, you'd know that Jill could not be reading or knitting with her eyes closed.

Finally, when a little visual information like the first letter is made available, you can narrow down your choices even further:

> Jill's eyes were closed.
> She was r_____ in the hammock.

She was probably rocking or resting.

Though I presented each source of information one at a time in a linear fashion, in actuality proficient readers quickly process all three at once. The reason we can read so fluently is not just because we recognize words instantly, but also because meaning and structure are continually driving us. While we read we are constantly anticipating what word could come next.

One goal for young readers is to use a balance of all three sources of information (see Figure 2–1). Research tells us that the brain can parallel process; we can do several things at once. "In Rumelhart's (1994) model of processing, the skilled brain can apparently work on different kinds of information simultaneously, which he described as a highly interactive parallel processing system" (Clay 2001, p. 124). In other words, we can hold the meaning and the language structure in our heads at the same time that we are examining the letters. For struggling readers, achieving this balance is difficult. Some children stick with one source of information and neglect the others. However, children who find it easy to focus on one type of information can be prompted to consider using another type of information (Clay 2001). Chapter 3 illustrates how teachers can help children use a balance of cues by modeling, supporting, and prompting for the source of information that the child is not using.

Figure 2–1
Sources of
Information That
Readers Use to
Figure Out Words
and Make Sense of
Print

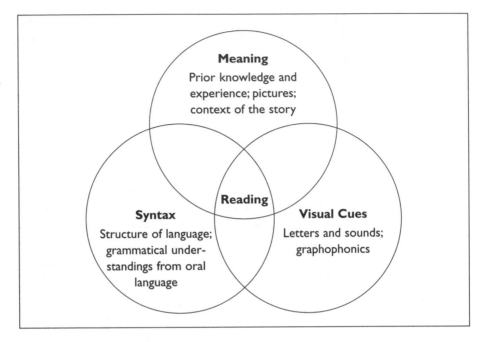

A common mistake that some teachers make is to prompt with the same source of information that the child is already using. For example, suppose the child is trying to read the word *find* in the sentence "I can't find him anywhere." The child notices the word *in* in the middle of *find* and continues to sound out using that information. Obviously, he won't arrive at the correct word. A teacher's first inclination is to prompt with more visual information, saying, "That's a short *i* sound. Try it with a long sound and see if that will work" or "You almost have it—try a different sound for that *i*." But the child was already using letters and sounds, visual information. Instead, the teacher should encourage the child to use a *balance of cues*, perhaps prompting with a meaning cue. "Remember, the little boy is looking everywhere for his dog. Keep that in mind as you try that sentence again." For early readers and many struggling readers, we need to prompt in support of balance when children are not showing evidence of using all sources of information.

To read more about using sources of information, see the following:

Clay, Marie. 1993b. *Reading Recovery: A Guidebook for Teachers in Training,* pp. 39–43.

Fountas, Irene C., and Gay Su Pinnell. 1996. *Guided Reading: Good First Teaching for All Children,* pp. 5–6.

Schulman, Mary, and Carleen Payne. 2000. *Guided Reading: Making It Work,* pp. 25–27.

Network of Strategies That Proficient Readers Use

It is difficult to ever know exactly what goes on in the head of a reader as he is engaged in the reading process. Most of the current information on strategies suggests that reading for meaning involves many in-the-head actions, which we cannot see but can infer are happening. The strategies presented in the circle in Figure 2–2 are adapted from the work of Clay (1991, 2001), Fountas and Pinnell (2001), Schulman (2006), Schulman and Payne (2000), Keene and Zimmerman (1997), and Harvey and Goudvis (2000).

One way to look at this circle chart is to temporarily divide these strategies into the word-solving or basic comprehension strategies, the top half of the circle, and the deeper comprehension strategies, the bottom half of the circle. (The division aids our understanding; ultimately we need to view them all together.) Fountas and Pinnell (2001) refer to the top strategies as

Figure 2–2
The Process of
Reading Chart

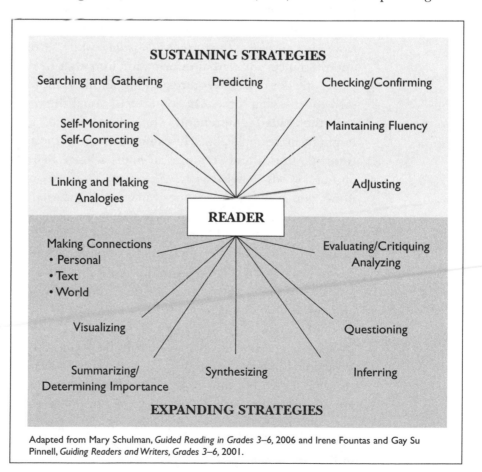

Adapted from Mary Schulman, *Guided Reading in Grades 3–6*, 2006 and Irene Fountas and Gay Su Pinnell, *Guiding Readers and Writers, Grades 3–6*, 2001.

"sustaining reading strategies" because they sustain the reader with text, helping him figure out the print and make sense of the text.

For example, when recognizing words, a reader might *search* for information from the letters and pictures; he *gathers* information from his background knowledge or from the context of the story; he *links* parts of unknown words with parts of words he does know; and he *predicts* what a word might be. A reader confronting an unknown word might also *cross-check* the meaning and structural information with the visual graphophonics cues to *confirm* a prediction. The reader is constantly keeping a check on himself by *self-monitoring*—does the word look right? Make sense? Sound right?

Fountas and Pinnell (2001) refer to the bottom half of the circle as the "expanding reading strategies" because these help a reader get beyond the literal level of meaning, expanding to a deeper underlying level of comprehension. A reader can *ask questions* of the text, *visualize,* or *make connections* to help himself stay engaged with what he is reading. He can *infer* beyond the text level to suggest the author's meaning or draw a conclusion. He can *pick out important information* while reading nonfiction texts and then incorporate that information into what he already knows.

Proficient readers require and use all these strategies, but not necessarily at the same time. On some texts, visualizing the information may help the reader comprehend, while on other texts making an inference might be more applicable. For example, in order for me to understand the futuristic worlds and creatures in many science fiction novels, I use the author's words to help me *visualize* quite often. However, when reading a nonfiction article on tornadoes I may use the *determining importance* strategy as I sort through which facts are the most crucial things I need to know in order to understand how tornadoes begin.

Many times a reader uses a combination of several strategies that overlap and intertwine. The important point is that these strategies have to be available to the reader so that she may draw upon them flexibly and fluently when she is stuck on a word or confused by a passage. Clay (2001) says we cannot teach a strategy but can only encourage students to be strategic by the way in which we teach. By paying careful attention to the struggling reader, examining running records or other assessment tools to see what she is not using or only partially using, teachers can point out relevant information with direct or indirect prompts. However, "if a teacher does not understand literacy processing, prompting will be hit or miss" (Clay 2001, p. 128). Clay's point confirms my emphasis on the importance of the *here's what* stage. We need to take a careful look to help us understand what a particular child who is struggling is doing as a reader. Then, by juxtaposing that information against what proficient readers do in the *so what* phase, we can plan effective instruction for that child.

All together these strategies compose a network in the head of the reader. I always worry about using literacy jargon, such as *network of strategies,* without careful explanation. Too much "teacher talk" (as my husband calls it) can be vague. I wouldn't want an overdose of literacy jargon to cause a teacher to give up on my text, so I want to make the idea of "network of strategies" accessible for everyone. Think of the word *network* for a minute. Early in my career I started a network group of reading teachers, who got together to share ideas and lessons we were modeling in classrooms. We worked together to solve literacy problems we encountered at our various schools. My husband, as chief financial officer (CFO) of the Smithsonian Institution, had a network group with other CFOs of universities and nonprofit organizations. As a network group they brought information together from various sources to share ways to solve problems. Like these two examples, the network of strategies in the head of the learner is there to help solve problems the reader encounters with print.

In the dictionary the word *network* is defined as "anything resembling a net in concept or form" or "a group or system of electronic components and connecting circuitry designed to function in a specific manner." Visualizing a net helps me picture the way these strategies are woven together. The second definition gives us a way to think about how this circle of strategies operates. The *function* they are supposed to perform is to help a person read and understand. The *connecting circuitry* means the strategies overlap and crisscross in many different ways. I once saw a presenter show a graphic of strategies (similar to Figure 2–2) on an overhead. She then shook that paper up and down and back and forth, to get us to imagine the fluidity and interconnectedness of these strategies as they form a working system in the head of a learner.

Another way to help teachers understand this network of strategies is to make an analogy to the Web. Way back when I was first getting my technology feet wet, I asked my husband, "But where *is* the World Wide Web?" He looked at me, exasperated, and waving his arms said, "It's just out there, in the air, and it's all connecting in lots and lots of ways." That's how I sometimes think of the network of strategies in the head of the reader, just "up there" in the brain, connecting and linking in various ways as the child problem-solves his way through text.

Figuring out how to help each struggling reader is a complex task, but one thing is for sure—it is profoundly related to this network of strategies.

To read more about the topic of network of strategies:

Schulman, Mary, and Carleen Payne. 2000. *Guided Reading: Making It Work*, pp. 28–32.

Pinnell, Gay Su, and Patricia Scharer. 2003. *Teaching for Comprehension in Reading, Grades K–2*, pp. 16–32.

Fountas, Irene C., and Gay Su Pinnell. 2001. *Guiding Readers and Writers, Grades 3–6*, pp. 302–321.

Keene, Ellin, and Susan Zimmerman. 1997. *Mosaic of Thought: Teaching Comprehension in a Reader's Workshop*, pp. 13–28.

Harvey, Stephanie, and Anne Goudvis. 2000. *Strategies That Work: Teaching Comprehension to Enhance Understanding*, pp. 3–26.

Although the reasons children struggle vary from child to child and we need to study the uniqueness of each child, *most are having trouble putting together the complex network of strategies needed to solve print and understand text* (Clay 2001). Struggling readers need teachers who understand reading as a process rather than as a collection of letters, sounds, and sight vocabulary.

A Comprehensive Literacy Environment

You do not have to be in a school with any one particular reading program in use in order to benefit from the ideas presented in this book. However, the way in which some classroom environments are organized and managed makes it easier for the teacher to find time to meet with children who are struggling. In order for you to take the most advantage of the lessons and techniques in this book, and because each struggling reader is unique and needs time with the teacher to address his specific needs, your classroom reading program needs to provide time and opportunity for reading to, with, and by students (Mooney 1990). A balanced literacy approach builds in time for meeting with small groups and individually with students.

Figure 2–3 shows a balanced literacy approach, which includes various reading and writing contexts. The line running diagonally across the block is meant to show how much input and support is coming from the teacher and how much responsibility the students must carry for doing the reading work. An effective reading program offers a balance of these four contexts—reading aloud, shared reading, guided reading, and independent reading. (A comprehensive literacy program also includes the writing contexts noted in Figure 2–3, but the scope of this text does not allow for elaboration on those.)

A balanced literacy approach does not mean an eclectic program with pieces from every method of teaching reading. *Balance* refers to having a balance in your program of *whose responsibility it is to do the reading work*. In other words, how much responsibility for figuring out the words and comprehending the meaning is the job of the teacher and how much of that

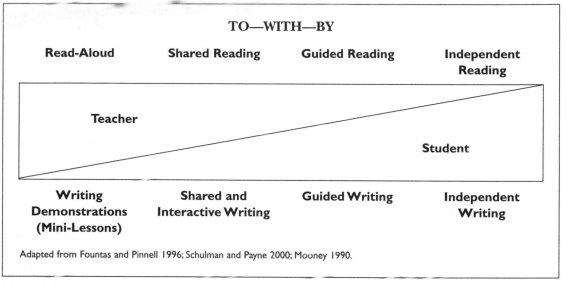

TO—WITH—BY

| Read-Aloud | Shared Reading | Guided Reading | Independent Reading |

Teacher

Student

| Writing Demonstrations (Mini-Lessons) | Shared and Interactive Writing | Guided Writing | Independent Writing |

Adapted from Fountas and Pinnell 1996; Schulman and Payne 2000; Mooney 1990.

Figure 2–3
Balanced Literacy
Approach

job belongs to the students? Each of the four contexts for reading—read-aloud time, shared reading, guided reading, and independent reading—provide different amounts of teacher support and different amounts of student responsibility. It is the variance of that support that leads to a successful learning environment. Children, especially struggling readers, need time for the following:

- Observing explicit modeling of reading strategies and behaviors
- Participating in shared demonstrations
- Practicing the strategies they are learning on material that is appropriately matched to their ability and interest, and when the teacher is still available for guided support
- Strengthening their system of strategies during individual reading time

Let's examine some classrooms that don't offer a balance. What if a classroom reading program overemphasizes reading aloud to the exclusion of the other contexts? I've heard teachers say, "I have too many learning disabled children and second language learners in my room who can't read the texts, so I do a lot of the reading with whole-class novels and the students follow along." These children are not getting the instruction they need. There isn't time provided for clear instruction in small groups on strategies these students are lacking. Nor is there enough practice time in texts that these students can handle on their own.

Another classroom may spend too much time on individualized reading to the exclusion of other contexts. Allowing students time to read, without any modeling or shared demonstrations on reading strategies, or any guided practice time, is also not sufficient. And yet I've heard teachers proclaim, "I just fill the room with books and let the kids read." Where's the instructional piece of this program? Where's the assessment piece? Where is the tailored instruction meeting the needs of individual struggling readers? The *balance* of the four parts of a reading program is there for a reason.

Description of Reading Components

As each context in the reading workshop is explained, note how much responsibility for doing the reading work falls on the teacher and how much is expected of the student. Also notice the instructional component of each context.

Read-Aloud Daily time is needed for the teacher to read aloud interesting books from a variety of genres and spanning diverse literature. These can be chapter books or well-written picture books; a mixture of both is preferred. The teacher would have most of the responsibility for the reading work in this context since she does the reading and the children listen. A small amount of the responsibility is handled by the students as they negotiate the meaning of the text together—perhaps turning and talking to discuss, pose questions, or make connections and predictions.

More often than not, the purpose of reading aloud to your students is to enjoy texts together, build a sense of community through shared literary experiences, and develop a reading history of common texts together as a class. But on occasion read-alouds can be used for instructional purposes. The teacher can model many of the strategies and behaviors that proficient readers use by doing a think-aloud with a picture book, poem, or excerpt from a chapter book. An interactive read-aloud lesson would involve the children more as they apply and practice the strategy that has just been modeled in the think-aloud.

Shared Reading The shared reading context usually involves the use of Big Books, poems on charts, or lifted text placed on the overhead projector. The text must be large enough for all to see. The teacher does the reading, carrying a lot of the responsibility, but the students can join in and do the reading with her when they feel comfortable doing so. With

To read more about the topic of balanced literacy classrooms, see the following:

Dorn, Linda, Cathy French, and Tammy Jones. 1998. *Apprenticeship to Literacy: Transitions Across Reading and Writing,* Chapters 1–8.

Schulman, Mary, and Carleen Payne. 2000. *Guided Reading: Making It Work,* Chapters 1–4.

Fountas, Irene C., and Gay Su Pinnell. 2001. *Guiding Readers and Writers, Grades 3–6,* Chapters 1–4.

Fountas, Irene C., and Gay Su Pinnell. 1996. *Guided Reading: Good First Teaching for All Children,* Chapters 3–5.

Mere, Cathy. 2005. *More Than Guided Reading: Finding the Right Instructional Mix, K–3,* Chapter 1.

Routman, Regie. 2003. *Reading Essentials: The Specifics You Need to Teach Reading Well,* Chapters 9–10.

young children the shared reading of Big Books and poems is first and foremost for enjoyment. On subsequent readings, however, when the children are very familiar with the text, the teacher may use it for instructional purposes. The focus of a shared reading demonstration can be any of the behaviors or strategies that readers use—predicting what a word might mean from its context, rereading or reading on, picking out important information, learning to use nonfiction features of print, visualizing, checking or confirming the punctuation cues, and so on. The teacher shares the reading work with the students as she guides them through the lesson.

Guided Reading Guided reading is small-group work intended to offer time for children to practice the reading skills and strategies they are learning. The focus of a guided reading lesson is matched to what this particular group of students needs in order to improve as readers. Much more of the responsibility for doing the reading work is given over to the students in this context as each child assumes the role of reader with his own copy of the text. The teacher introduces the text, does a book introduction, and then has a brief discussion with the students. The focus of the lesson is made clear to the students. The texts are read by each child individually, rather than by round-robin reading. The teacher has matched each child to an appropriate text within the range of her ability in guided reading, which makes it possible for the children to be successful on their own. As they read, the children draw upon their system of strategies to figure out words and understand the text. The teacher is available for scaffolding and prompting. (Other children in the class would be involved in literacy centers or worthwhile literacy tasks to permit the teacher time to work with small groups.)

Individual Reading Children need time and opportunity to put their system of strategies to work. Time needs to be provided daily for independent reading. Each child in primary grades might have a book box filled with familiar texts—some self-selected, but many from guided reading lessons. In upper grades children also have texts handy that they are presently reading, some self-selected and some teacher selected. When children are reading individually (or sometimes buddy reading), the teacher is freed up to work with individual children, to assess with running records or individualized conferences, or to do some explicit one-on-one teaching with struggling readers.

Levels of Texts

Throughout the book I describe many struggling readers between kindergarten and grade five. I refer to each of them using one of the following words: *emergent, progressing, transitional, developing, independent,* and *fluent.* In order for teachers to understand the type of reader I am referring to, I have included a chart comparing levels of texts (see Figure 2–4). This chart is adapted from *Guided Reading: Making It Work* (2000) by Mary Schulman and Carleen Payne. The chart offers comparisons to text gradient systems used by others—a general basal reader series, Fountas and Pinnell's lettering series, the Reading Recovery numbering system, and Developmental Reading Assessment Tests (DRA) levels. The chart is intended to give teachers a sense of the reader being described in each situation. Teachers will be familiar with at least one of the systems offered.

COMPARISON CHART OF LEVELED TEXTS

Type of Reader	Reading Recovery Levels	Fountas and Pinnell Levels	Basal Reading Levels	DRA Test Levels
Emergent	1	A	Readiness	A, 1, 2
	2	B		
	3	C	Preprimer	3
	4			
	5	D		4
	6			
Progressing	7	E		
	8			6–8
	9	F	Primer	10
	10			
	11	G		12
Transitional	12		Grade 1	
	13	H		14
	14			
	15	I		16
	16			
Developing	17			
	18	J	Grade 2	18–20
	19			
	20	K		
Independent		L		24–28
		M		
Fluent		N	Grade 3	30
		O		
		P		34–38
		Q	Grade 4	40
		R		
		S	Grade 5	44

Adapted from Schulman and Payne, 2000. *Guided Reading: Making It Work.* New York: Scholastic.

Figure 2–4
Comparison Chart
of Leveled Texts

CHAPTER 3

Active Participation

When working with a group of teachers, I often ask, "What kind of reader would you like to see emerge from your classroom by the end of the school year?" The answers that surface are similar, whether the group consists of primary teachers, upper-elementary teachers, or a combination of both. Most say they hope for children who:

- like reading;
- choose to read at home and not just in school;
- read from a variety of genres;
- read fluently;
- understand what they read;
- pay attention to what they read;
- know ways to "fix up" when an error has been made.

The answer that always rises to the top after some discussion is "children who have effective ways to solve problems when they are stuck." Keep in mind that children can get stuck on a word (one they are not able to figure out or one they can say but whose meaning escapes them) or on a passage (they may read a whole paragraph, page, or story and not under-stand what they read). When we say we want children to be problem solvers, we mean that they should have strategic actions they can perform to figure out words and gain meaning from the text; actions for helping themselves when they are stuck. Marie Clay (1993b) talks about three kinds of strategies: ones for solving words, ones for detecting and correct-ing errors, and ones for maintaining fluency and comprehension.

Being a problem solver means actively initiating the use of strategies. Proficient readers *take action* when they become stuck; they use multiple strategies at the point of difficulty. Proficient readers use strategies *flexibly,* in a variety of ways and combinations. And proficient readers are *fluent* with their use of strategies, employing them immediately and automati-cally. As stated earlier, we cannot put the reading process into the head of the learner; the child is the one who builds his network of strategies. We can only model, support, prompt, and then back off slowly as the child begins to use those strategies.

Encouraging active participation in the reading process right from the beginning is an important step in supporting readers who struggle (Askew and Fountas 1996). We have all known a child who sits and does nothing when he comes to an unknown word. We make up various reasons about why he responds this way—he's shy, he's not a risk taker, his mom always gives him the word at home, his last year's teacher was afraid he would cry or get frustrated so she often jumped in too quickly, or he never learned enough phonics. Buying into these excuses will only misdirect our ener-gies away from helping that child become an active participant in con-structing his network of strategies.

Passive behavior is not limited to readers who make no attempts at fig-uring out words. Many upper-elementary readers who read the words but don't understand what they read have also been known to do nothing about their confusion or lack of comprehension. Some try to hide it, slink-ing down in their seats, hoping not to be called on. Others try to fake it; they agree with or rephrase what another child said in the group discus-sion. Some aren't even aware of when they comprehend and when they don't. And still others boldly announce, "I did so read it all. I just didn't understand any of it!" (Tovani 2000).

When confronted with a passive reader, whether at the word level or the text level, we need to be proactive, recognizing that it's time to do some serious teaching to help the child become an active participant in constructing a system of strategies for the meaning-making process called reading. In this chapter we look first at Yessica as I take her through the framework of *here's what, so what, now what,* and *then what.* Then I address some related issues—setting the tone in your classroom for active participation, prompting for a balance of all sources of information, and teaching students to actively use the strategic behaviors of rereading and reading ahead. Included is information on using scaffolding and encouraging multiple attempts. And finally, the chapter examines the importance of providing opportunities to strengthen the system of strategies by using it.

Yessica's Story: A Beginning Reader Learns to Actively Search and Link

Yessica was a native Spanish speaker who had been learning English since she started school. Though her kindergarten program was only a half day, her teacher used a balanced literacy approach—lots of reading aloud; shared reading experiences with Big Books, poems, and songs; shared and interactive writing; writing workshop; independent book-box reading time; and literacy centers. This environment provided Yessica with lots of opportunities for talk, total immersion in print, and continued demonstrations of real reading and writing. As a result, Yessica began to pick up English quite naturally, gaining lots of social language.

By the beginning of first grade, Yessica could identify more than half of the upper- and lowercase letters. She also knew a few sounds or a word that began with about one-third of the letters. And she showed evidence of one-to-one matching. But, as is typical for many second language learners, Yessica's English vocabulary was limited. She knew one word for something (happy), but not several (joyful, gay, glad, thrilled). Or she knew the names of a few animals in English (cat, dog, bird, snake) but not the less common ones (lizard, leopard, raccoon, seal).

During Yessica's first-grade year her teacher, Laura McDonnell, became concerned around November. She felt that Yessica was not progressing in reading compared with other children who began at about the same level. She noticed that Yessica was still in early emergent texts while others had moved on and that she was using avoidance tactics when it came time to read. Laura called me in for a consultation and asked for my advice.

Here's What

I began by listening to Yessica read her familiar books from her book box, those the teacher had introduced to her. I also introduced new books to

Yessica on two different days. These were beginning emergent books with patterned texts, consistent placement of print, and illustrations that provided high support and contained familiar objects and actions.

Examples: Look at the zebra.
Look at the tiger.
Look at the bear.

I can read the cereal box.
I can read the stop sign.
I can read the birthday card.
I can read the newspaper.

The last word in the sentence always connected to the illustration, which provides a very large clue for English-speaking children. However, for second language learners that picture is not always enough. Yessica was struggling to memorize all these new English labels—names of animals, foods, toys, vehicles, actions, and so on.

I looked over some of the running records that the classroom teacher had taken in the past weeks and took a few of my own. I noticed a pattern in Yessica's behavior when she came to an unknown word. First she waited a moment (indicated by a *w* written above the line). Then she looked at the ceiling, repeatedly tapping her forehead and saying, "Um, um, um." She was trying desperately to remember the English word for what was in the picture. She knew the meaning behind the unknown word; she just couldn't come up with the English label for it. Eventually Laura or I told her the word (indicated by a *T* written below the line).

w /	w /	w /
hippo T	potatoes T	kangaroo T

w /	w /
sign T	newspaper T

I talked with Laura about what I noticed. She concurred, saying, "I know. There's so much new vocabulary in these books. I feel like I have to help her with all those new English words." I, too, found myself being sympathetic to Yessica's dilemma. But careful reflection and talking together made us realize that our sympathy was misguided. We were helping to the point of creating a passive reader, one who was beginning to think that reading was a matter of just remembering the words.

So What

Sometimes it's important to look at our own actions to really understand what is blocking a child's progress. Laura and I discovered we were creating a dependency situation; Yessica knew we'd come to her rescue eventually. My knowledge of reading process and of teaching beginning readers told me that it was important to get the learner to be an active participant in problem solving as quickly as possible (Askew and Fountas 1998; Clay 1993b). Even if Yessica couldn't remember the word, there were other strategic actions she could be trying. Becoming a reader doesn't mean just reading the words accurately; at times it also means taking on a strategy or part of a strategy. Only with the development of strategic actions would Yessica begin to construct the process of reading on her own.

Observing Yessica's reading, analyzing running records, and conferring with Laura led me to make some decisions about instruction. Yessica needed to learn how to look at print in a way that would help her. She needed to learn *where to look:* search the beginning letter. In addition Yessica needed to learn *what to do with what she saw:* link to another word that she knew that starts with the same letter. Then I had to teach her how to reread and try again. I thought about how I would demonstrate this to Yessica, what explicit language I would use, and how I would get her to try it. I shared all of this with Laura and invited her to watch my next teaching encounter with Yessica.

Now What

After I introduced a new book to Yessica, she began to read the text. I was right by her side, ready for opportunities to model and prompt. As Laura watched me working, here is what she observed when Yessica got stuck on the word *tiger.*

Yessica: Um, um, um . . . (*tapping her forehead*)
Pat: You're stuck on that word, aren't you? I don't want you to look at the ceiling, Yessica, that's not helping you. Let me show you something you can do when you're stuck.
Yessica: (*looks at Pat and then down at the book*)
Pat: Here's where I want you to look. I want you to find that tricky word and put your finger right here, under the first letter. (*I take Yessica's finger to the beginning of the word.*) Now, what letter is that?
Yessica: *T.*

Pat: Right, it is *t*. Now think of your ABC book. Do you know a word that starts with *t*?

Yessica: *Table?*

Pat: Yes, *table* does start with a *t,* just like the word in this book. So here's what you can do if you're stuck. You can get your finger under that first letter and think of something that starts like that. Then go back and try this part again, but when you get to that tricky word, I want you to make that sound, just like at the beginning of *table,* OK? Here, watch me try it. (*I demonstrate exactly what I just explained to Yessica. When I get to the tricky word, I emphasize the beginning sound as I say the word* tiger.)

This is an example of an explicit demonstration. I showed Yessica exactly what I wanted her to do the next time she gets stuck. I may have to explain it one or two more times, and again have her watch me do it or we'll try a few times together.

In referring to similar teacher demonstrations, Tharp and Gallimore write, "The child may have very limited understanding of the situation, the task, or the goal to be achieved" (1988, p. 33). The teacher understands how this strategic action will eventually help the child, but the child doesn't. The teaching is "future oriented" (Lyons 2003), aimed at getting the student to eventually use all three sources of information to figure out words. The child's response is usually imitative at this point (Tharp and Gallimore 1988).

I continued to support Yessica as she tried the new behavior. Over the course of this lesson and the next, I gradually started backing off and let Yessica take over some of the responsibility. Eventually she didn't need me to model it anymore; she actively tried it on her own after a prompt. Here is what the interaction sounded like later:

Pat: You show me where to look this time.

Yessica: (*points to the first letter and makes that sound*)

Pat: Good. I like the way you thought about how this word can start. Now let's go back and read that sentence together and make that sound when we get there. Remember to keep thinking about what that word might be.

I did this together with Yessica several times. Although I still provided the word, she was learning to try something that would eventually help her.

Over the next few days, both Laura and I worked with Yessica on this particular strategic action: searching for the first letter, linking the letter with another word that starts like that, going back and rereading the sentence, and getting that first sound out when she gets to the unknown word. Sometimes I gave two choices for the unknown word, saying, "Is it *seal* or *whale*?" This causes Yessica to do some of the reading work as she decides between the two words. To do this she must use first-letter information.

With time and practice, the student gets faster and faster as she takes over the strategic action. She is starting to realize how this tool will help her figure out words in the text. The process doesn't always result in accuracy (getting the word), but Yessica is no longer tapping her forehead, looking at the ceiling. Here is a typical example of what her running records were starting to show:

Yessica: The birds are sssss/sad/ _____
                             safe
Text: The birds are safe.

Notice how Yessica is doing so much more than just waiting for someone to tell her the word. She is actively taking the initiative to solve the word. Yessica tried the first sound very quickly, and then thought about the story and put in a word that could show how the birds might be feeling. First, she used visual information (letter sound *s*), then she combined the letter/sound knowledge with meaningful information to make a good prediction (*sad*). This is great reading work! And because I want her to continue to actively search and try words that make sense, I compliment her. "I like the way you are always checking the first letter and thinking about what would make sense." At this point, it's not important that she read the word *safe* correctly. I can go back to that at a later time. For right now, I want her to know that her active participation in attempting to solve this word is what matters.

Next it was time to back off the amount of help I was giving Yessica so that she could fully take over that strategic activity and use it all on her own. This is usually done by changing what you say. Early on, I said things like, "Put your finger under that first letter" or "OK, now go back and reread." These prompts reminded Yessica of exactly what to do. Over time, I switched to saying things like, "What can you try?" or "Think about something you can do that might help you here." These prompts encouraged Yessica to take the initiative to try the strategic behavior we had been working on.

Then What

I continued to watch Yessica, and soon it became evident that she was using the strategic action automatically when she became stuck, without any reminders from me. By checking her running records, I saw how much it was working for her (SC stands for self-correction).

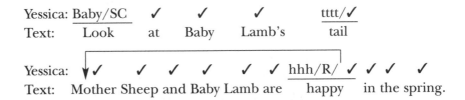

When you find that the child has taken over the strategy as Yessica had done, it's always good to continue reinforcing it for a while. To reinforce it, you praise it, name what it is the child did, and tell her that it's helping. For example, I said to her, "Wow, what you did there was great! You were thinking about how Mother Sheep and Baby Lamb were feeling, weren't you? And then you got your mouth ready for that first sound. When you went back and read it again, that word *happy* just popped right out of your mouth! That really helped you, Yessica. I hope you keep doing that as a reader. It's a good thing to try when you're stuck."

Throughout this whole teaching focus, Laura and I never stopped talking about the meaning of stories with this student. Emphasis on reading for meaning was always at the forefront. We discussed the story line before and after reading. Our specific teaching points were aimed at helping Yessica become a more active participant in figuring out words. Instead of just trying to remember words, we aimed our teaching at helping her use some visual information. She had some letter/sound knowledge, but did not know how to use that knowledge to help her solve words.

All this took place in a matter of four or five days. The classroom teacher and I knew it was time to cycle back to the *here's what* phase and see what else Yessica needed to be taught.

The main point here is that a teacher is always looking for specific strategies and behaviors that can help the child become a better reader. We are not just "doing the book" to get another book into her book box. Rather, time spent with a struggling reader has an instructional focus. When we teach for strategies we are helping children construct a repertoire of ways to figure out words and understand text. We continue with responsive teaching, varying our supports in response to what the child says and does. Then we gradually release the responsibility all the way to independence, when the children can use the strategies and behaviors on their own.

Teaching reading is not always about accuracy, getting the word right. At times teaching is focused on getting the child to *take on* a strategy or part of a strategy. Learning a strategy, a way to attempt to solve a problem, sometimes takes precedence over item knowledge, like learning a word or a sound. "Learning 'how to do something' is powerful learning" (Clay 2001). When we teach for strategies we are teaching ways to solve problems that students can use on another day in another situation. Readers need to own this network of strategies, using part or parts of it when a need arises.

Setting the Tone for Active Participation

It's no secret that children learn to value what their teacher emphasizes in the classroom. Teachers who push for speed and accuracy, for example, by having children time themselves on passages, will often produce children who value fast reading and correct word calling over comprehension. Classrooms where reading time comprises practicing words on flash cards, sounding out words, and isolated phonics activities might yield children who believe that reading is only about getting the words right. Likewise, teachers who use language to show that they value persistence with problem solving, reading for meaning, and self-monitoring behaviors will encourage children to strive to acquire these strategies. It is the teacher, by her choice of what to praise and what instructional points to use, who sets that tone. The way in which we teach can either foster active participation or hinder it (Clay 1991).

As the reading teacher at Garfield Elementary School, I had the honor one year of working with Noel Naylor, then a first-grade classroom teacher and now a Reading Recovery trainer in our district. Noel developed a wonderful community among her students; each child respected and valued the contributions of every other student in the room. Noel was also a master at setting the tone for what she valued as good reading work. One day I was walking Melody, my Reading Recovery student, back to her classroom and I said, "You sure have a lot of great readers in your class, don't you?" Melody answered by naming several "great readers." To my surprise, four out of five were Reading Recovery students (children who have been identified as at-risk and were receiving daily early intervention). I decided to pursue her train of thought and asked, "So what makes Mustafa such a great reader?" She answered, "He checks and goes back when he's stuck." "And what else?" I asked. "Well," she said, "he always likes the book to make sense." It's obvious that Melody was getting messages from her teacher about what was important for becoming a proficient reader.

Think about the tone you are setting in your classroom by reflecting on the following questions:

- Are you praising only when children are 100 percent accurate or are you bringing children's attention to occasions when a student had some difficulty but actively tried several different ways to rectify the problem?
- Are you saying, "Good job," but not being specific about what you are praising this child for?
- Does your feedback reinforce a particular action, such as stopping to check if you were making sense or rereading the line to fix an error?
- Are you explicitly modeling strategies and behaviors that proficient readers use to solve problems, thus showing that readers *are* active participants?
- Are you using shared reading with Big Books or doing shared demonstrations with lifted text on the overhead, giving students opportunities to suggest or initiate strategic actions?

We all send hidden messages to children about what reading is for and what readers do through our praise and our emphasis during instruction.

The incident with Melody happened several years ago. Since that time I've become more watchful of the language I use to describe readers. For example, if there are "great readers," then there must be "bad readers," so I try not to label readers that way. Several teachers and I recently read and discussed Peter Johnston's remarkable book *Choice Words: How Our Language Affects Children's Learning*. Johnston encourages teachers to reflect on the language we use daily as we interact with children. He says, "A good-bad continuum is not the only way to name readers and writers" (2004, p. 19). Kathleen Fay, a colleague who also read the book, reminds us, "when we teach in other subject areas we often say, 'that's what scientists do' or 'that's what artists do,' so why do we change that when talking about readers?" As a result of the discussions around Johnston's book, many of us have changed our speech to "This is what readers do; readers check to make sure they are making sense; readers check the print to see if there is a part of the word they know; readers make pictures in their minds," and so on.

Actively Using All Sources of Information

Chapter 2 explains how readers, when stuck on an unknown word, can draw information from three sources—meaning, structure, and visual cues. Some struggling readers overly depend on one source of information while neglecting others. Stephanie was one such child who was, as Clay says, "over-committed" to the idea that reading is about sounding out. She had been to a private kindergarten where phonics was stressed. Sounding out was so engrained in Stephanie that she would often persist with it even when it wasn't helping her at all. My job was to help her realize that there are other kinds of information she could be taking into account. I wanted her to actively use all the information available to her and not persist with sounding out alone.

Stephanie: (*reading from a text about a child who got hurt on the playground*) "The children went to the teacher. They said, 'Tracy has a s-o-r-e . . .'" (*Stephanie tries the word* sore *by sounding each of the letters in a variety of ways, but to no avail.*)

Pat: I see you are using some of those sounds to try to help you figure out that word, Stephanie. Let me show you something else you can try here. (*I cover over the sentence with my hand to bring Stephanie's attention to me and what I'm saying.*) I want you to think about the story. Tell me what happened to Tracy.

Stephanie: She fell on the playground. She's bleeding.

Pat: You're right. Her knee must really hurt. Did you ever fall down and get a bruise or a sore on your leg?

Stephanie: I fell off the swing and cut my elbow right here.

Pat: Keep that in mind, about Tracy getting hurt just like you, when you try this page again.

Stephanie was originally using visual information only, I prompted her with something meaningful. She needed to get the meaning of what was happening in the story back into her head. Spending too much time trying to decode a word solely with visual information will often cause loss of meaning. As a reader, Stephanie does not yet have both meaning and visual information working together.

Let's look at another example of a teacher prompting for balance. Jesse, another emergent reader, is the direct opposite of Stephanie in how he approaches new words. Jesse has lots of background knowledge and depends heavily on meaning and structure to carry him. He looks as little as possible at the visual information—the letters and sounds. He relies only on the pictures, his personal experiences, and his memory of what the book is about.

Jesse: "I went to the zoo. I saw a porpoise." [text word: *dolphin*]

Teacher: That might be a porpoise. Or it might be a seal or a dolphin or a walrus. How can you tell?

Jesse: Because I know that's what a porpoise's nose looks like. (*He is still using only the picture and his background knowledge to help him.*)

Teacher: You're right. The picture is one way to help you. But how do you know that word says "porpoise" and not "dolphin"? Dolphins and porpoises look alike. (*The teacher is hoping he'll know he has to check the first letter.*)

Jesse: I just know.

Teacher: Let me show you a way you can check *the word* to decide if this book says *porpoise* or *dolphin*. (*The teacher continues by showing him the first-letter information.*)

Consider the parts of responsive teaching discussed in Chapter 1—modeling, scaffolding, prompting, backing off, and reinforcing. In this example, the teacher began the interaction with prompting when she asked, "How can you tell?" But when she realized that Jesse did not know how to check his prediction, she knew she must go to the modeling level to explicitly instruct him. That's responsive teaching. Based on what the child did, the teacher adjusted her amount of support.

We expect children who are just beginning to learn to read, like Jesse, to predict a word from the illustration or their background knowledge. But then we need to encourage them to check their prediction by using the letters of the word, usually just the first letter at this emergent level. Then the child either continues reading because he has confirmed that he is correct or he makes another attempt, rearranging his prediction. Jesse needed his teacher to help him confirm or rearrange his prediction with visual information. If the teacher maintains this strategy as her teaching focus for a while, Jesse will learn a way to check on his predictions by himself.

What accounts for the fact that Jesse wanted to invent text and leave it at that? Kindergarten children, and even toddlers at home, turn the pages of a book making up the story. This is perfectly appropriate, letting children feel like readers. As young children invent text, we are accepting their approximations of how this book could sound. Later, as they begin to read emergent-level texts, we still encourage children to use the pictures as one means of figuring out the print. Again, the pictures are part of the meaning, so this is still appropriate. But as soon as the reader shows that he can handle voice-to-print matching, it's time to start developing additional ways to figure out the print and confirm predictions. As the gradient of text increases, the picture support will start to diminish. Yet some children, like Jesse, are content continuing to invent, overly depending on only one source of information. It is our job to help him add to his use of meaning by showing him how the letters and sounds can help him.

Checking on whether Jesse is taking control of the confirming behavior (checking his prediction with some letter information), we might want to ask a question even when he gets a word correct. For example, when Jesse reads, "Father Bear went down to the river" correctly, the teacher might ask, "How do you know that word was *river,* and not *lake* or *pond?*" If he still answers with only picture information, such as "Because a lake would be bigger and this looks like a river," then the teacher knows she has more work to do.

Actively Initiating Strategic Behaviors

Children need not only to learn to use a balance of all the sources of information, but also to actively initiate several strategic behaviors. *Learning to reread* a sentence or part of a sentence is one such behavior. Rereading is done for many reasons. Sometimes a child rereads to check to make sure the word he predicted looked right. Sometimes rereading is used to check intonation based on a mark of punctuation. Or sometimes a child can learn to reread a sentence when he becomes stuck on a word. In this sense, the rereading helps the child *gather* information so that he can then make a prediction for the unknown word. Every once in a while we come across a child who rereads out of habit, but is not doing the thinking that is supposed to accompany the rereading.

Kathleen Fay, a reading teacher, told me a story of a student, Martin, who did exactly that. Martin would latch onto the phrase that preceded the unknown word and continually repeat the phrase over and over, rapidly, almost like a parrot. The rereading seemed to do nothing to help him predict the next word because he rarely made an attempt. She talked with another teacher, Nancy Kurtz, to discuss what to do. Their conversation went something like this.

Kathleen: I thought rereading was supposed to help kids. I've been suggesting that Martin try that when he's stuck, but it doesn't seem to be helping him.

Nancy: Rereading is just a behavior, not a strategy. Behaviors, like rereading, are things we can see the child doing. Strategies are the in-the-head thinking. Usually the behaviors hint at what is going on in the head of the child. But in this case it seems Martin is using the behavior of rereading, but he's not doing the strategy work, the thinking that goes along with it.

Kathleen: Yes, that could be it. It's like a bad habit. He's rereading in a rote manner but not using it to figure out the unknown word that stopped him in the first place.

Nancy: The behavior of rereading is a way to help a child *search and gather* meaning from the beginning of the sentence so that he can then *predict* the next word. Martin doesn't realize that the rereading is meant to put the meaning of the sentence back in his head so that he can then make an attempt at what that next word might be.

As Nancy and Kathleen talked they decided Kathleen should go back and teach the strategy of gathering information and predicting. She needed to be explicit with Martin about what he's thinking as he rereads. "Be thinking about what would make sense here and start with that letter." Talking with colleagues about a specific problem concerning a struggling reader helps us sort out the difficulty that a child is having. Kathleen's conversation with Nancy helped focus her teaching for Martin.

Another strategic behavior that we can teach a child to actively initiate is *reading on.* Although rereading is encouraged with emergent-level texts, teaching about reading past the unknown word and then coming back is usually not effective until the child is reading in progressing- or transitional-level texts. I noticed that Christie, a struggling third grader reading in transitional-level texts, depended mostly on visual information, but occasionally used some meaning and structural information when stuck on a word. She would reread a sentence to solve a word, but she never skipped the word, read ahead, and then came back. I decided to teach her how to do this.

First, I thought aloud, demonstrating how a reader would try reading on and coming back. As I read past the word I thought aloud about what this tricky word could be, what would make sense. Then we tried this method on a few words together. Once Christie took partial control of the technique, I encouraged her to practice using that idea on her own on subsequent pages in the book. I said, "Go ahead and try that trick of reading on and coming back by yourself this time." Whenever it worked for her, I would reinforce the technique, saying, "You see how well that worked for you. Because you read the rest of the sentence, it gave you an idea of what word would make sense there." By the last few pages of the text, I had backed off enough and merely tapped on the table as a reminder. I told her, "I think you know how to do this on your own now. I'm not going to keep reminding you to read past the word. If you forget to try it, I'll just tap on the table." Eventually even the tapping was not needed. This is an example of backing off support, turning more of the responsibility over to the student.

Using Scaffolds to Support Children's Active Participation

Tapping on the table is a technique used to scaffold a child. Scaffolds can be put in place to help a child remember to activate strategies or behaviors. All scaffolds are meant to be taken down at some point, just like the scaffold you might construct to support you as you paint a ceiling (Wood, Bruner, and Ross 1976).

Like Yessica in the framework example, many children do nothing at the point of difficulty. For beginning struggling readers who are not making any attempts at word solving, I often use picture symbols as scaffolds. The symbols (see Figure 3–1) represent various strategic actions:

- Symbol 1 means, "Check the picture."
- Symbol 2 means, "Think about the story."
- Symbol 3 means, "Go back and reread."
- Symbol 4 means, "Check the first letter."

Figure 3–1
Picture Symbol Scaffolds

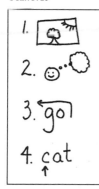

Each of these can be modeled in shared reading so that the children understand what the symbols mean before they are used one-on-one with a child. It is amazing to see a passive child (who usually waits for someone to give him the word) all of a sudden become active as I gently slide this card over toward him when he's stuck. Upon seeing the card, it's as if he wakes up and a voice in his head says, "Oh, yeah, I have to try something."

On other occasions I have used the card to reinforce a strategic behavior or suggest another way to attempt an unknown word. While touching one of the symbols on the card, I might say:

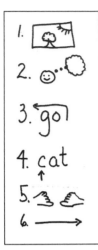

Figure 3–2
More Picture
Symbol Scaffolds

● "Wow, I saw you checking that picture. That's really helping you today."
● "I see you checking that first letter a lot. You are really doing well at getting your mouth ready for that first sound, but I'd like you to reread also. When you go back and reread and then make that sound, it might help you more."

Later, when the child is reading progressing-level texts, I add two more symbols (see Figure 3–2):

● Symbol 5 means, "Use your thumbs to find a part of the word that could help you."
● Symbol 6 means, "Read ahead and come back."

Tharp and Gallimore comment that scaffolding "does not involve simplifying the task; it holds the task difficulty constant while simplifying the child's role" (1988, p. 33). The child is still faced with the difficulty of figuring out a word, but the picture symbols simplify the child's role by reminding him of something he could try. They take the place of verbal reminders for the child. I provide them as a means of assistance, but after a time they need to be taken away. The goal is that these ideas (using the picture to gather meaning, checking the first letters or parts of the word, thinking about the story, and rereading or reading ahead to gather more information) become part of the child's thinking. As soon as you see the child trying these things without needing the card, remove it from sight. If it's not removed, the card may actually slow down the child's processing.

Having a list of picture cues in every child's reading folder or pasted to each book box but never talking about them in a teacher/child interaction is a waste of paper. Teachers should be sure that they are actually *using* the scaffolds with the children who need them. Some children can rattle off what each picture cue means, but this is not the goal. It is more important that we are able to observe whether the child has internalized their use.

Any form of scaffolding should be temporary. The danger is in turning your scaffolds (like the pictures in Figure 3–2) into some sort of orthodoxy. I shudder when I see these picture cues on charts hanging all over a school. I am reminded of an article Donald Graves (1984) wrote called "The Enemy Is Orthodoxy." In it, he warns teachers against taking the writer's process and turning it into a lockstep system—brainstorming, drafting, revising, editing, and publishing, as if we teach children to do the first on Monday, the next on Tuesday, and so forth. These picture scaffolds that I'm suggesting are meant to support children as they begin to construct a repertoire of strategies for figuring out words. We can't turn them into a mindless linear routine. A network of strategies, as discussed in Chapter 2, does not function in this way. Reading process is not ritualistic. Rather than a linear process, the strategies become part of a network in the reader's head. The reader draws upon the strategies in different ways in different situations, flexibly and fluently.

Multiple Attempts

I am always on the lookout for whether children are making multiple attempts to solve unknown words. In other words, when faced with some difficulty, the child tries one thing; if that doesn't work, she tries something else, and so forth. When Yessica was stuck on the word *safe,* she first sounded the *s* and then tried the word *sad.* This shows she was beginning to integrate the sources of information by trying some visual information first and then adding meaningful and structural information to make a prediction. Even though she did not read the word *safe* correctly, she was still showing us that she is willing to make multiple attempts.

One day, while reading with Sable, I took note of how quickly a system of strategies could operate for a child. The book told of the character's experience being sick and how a letter from friends cheered her up. In one part, the text went something like this:

When I was sick, I couldn't go out to play.
When I was sick, I felt tired all day.

On the word *tired,* Sable's problem solving was so quick I almost missed it. She made a quick *t* sound, then said, "tied" and then said, "tired." When I analyzed that, I inferred (1) that she used her phonics information quickly to produce the first letter sound; (2) that she used more visual information, trying more letter sounds, perhaps checked the end letters, to get to the word *tied;* and (3) that she then thought about the girl being sick and saw the picture of the girl lying in bed (meaningful information), which helped her quickly change her prediction of *tied* to *tired.* Though my interpretation takes minutes to explain, what Sable did actually took a fraction of a second. A network of strategies functioning well is practically automatic.

Some may ask, "Why bother to infer and analyze all that, if she read the word correctly so quickly?" The answer is that it helps me understand

Sable's processing. I need to know if she is using a balance of sources of information so that it can inform my instruction. It's not important for Sable to be able to explain what happened there, but it is important for me to understand it. I observe her running records for evidence of multiple attempts at solving words in different ways.

I also look to see if she is cross-checking. Readers cross-check by first using one source of information to predict a word and then checking or confirming their prediction with another source. For example, a child might predict an unknown word such as *water* (using meaning and structure), then check the first letter (using visual information) and change it to *river.* Or vice versa: a reader could predict the word *take* by using visual information and then cross-check with meaningful information to change the word to *talk.*

When focusing my teaching on a specific strategic activity for a child, I constantly look to see if the child is starting to use that without any prompting from me. Remember Stephanie earlier in this chapter, who was overcommitted to sounding out words? I worked hard to teach her how to better use meaningful information. Then I needed to observe in her running records whether she was doing that on her own.

The first time I saw evidence of her making multiple attempts, shifting from sounding out to something meaningful, she was reading, "The monkey was too naughty." When she got to the word *naughty* she first tried sounding every letter, but then said, "wild." I made a point of going back to that place after the running record was completed to praise her.

Stephanie needed to know that what she did was great reading work. There will not always be a teacher by her side to help with unknown words. Stephanie needs to become flexible enough to know that if sounding out is not helping her get the word quickly, then she needs to try something else, such as thinking about what might make sense. In order for the story to continue to make sense, she needs to be willing to let go of sounding out to substitute a word that would work in that instance.

Putting the Strategy System to Work

Who would argue with the fact that practicing something newly learned helps that skill develop? When I took tennis lessons, my coach taught me various techniques that would improve my game—get to the ball quickly, step into the ball when you swing, follow through on your swing, keep your eye on the ball, and so on. The things the coach said to me soon became part of my internal speech. As I was running to the ball, I could hear his voice in my head saying, "Get your racket back, get ready to step into it." Eventually I didn't have to say it to myself, I just did it! The only way I got to become a better tennis player was to actually play—and put the whole system together. Similarly, children who are learning to read need to put their system to work too, just like the tennis player.

When a child's network of strategies is beginning to form (some say it is "under construction"), the child needs opportunities to put that strategy system to work. Two of the best times for teachers to provide these opportunities are during guided reading and independent reading.

During guided reading, teachers provide students with books that are just right for them, that are not too hard or too easy. There should be enough challenge in those books so that the child has to use her network of strategies to figure out some words and work at constructing meaning, but at the same time has enough supports to allow her to read some passages smoothly. Although the teacher does a book introduction at the start of the guided reading lesson to help the child be successful with the book, that doesn't necessarily mean that the child will read it with 100 percent accuracy. The teacher leaves some work for the child to do. The child then reads the book on her own, perhaps with some prompting or support from the teacher. The teacher's prompts of "Are you right?" "Does that make sense?" "Read ahead and see if that helps you with the tricky word" soon become part of the inner speech in the head of the child. The child's inner speech eventually becomes inner thought, which is quicker and more automatic (Lyons 2003.)

The books that the child reads in guided reading are placed in his book box so that he can reread them during independent reading time. These repeated readings give the child more practice time using his system of strategies. The more opportunities a student has to put his system to work, the faster, stronger, and more efficient that system becomes. Marie Clay (2001) says that "frequent successful problem solving" helps strengthen the system.

When children are given time to practice using their system of strategies, their processing abilities eventually speed up. Let's look at a line that a child might be reading:

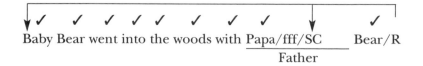

The child first reads the word *Father* as *Papa* and completes the sentence. But then the child stops. There's some dissonance in her head as she notices the first letter of the word *Father.* She hesitates. Then she goes all the way back to the beginning of the sentence, rereads, and, when she gets to the word *Father,* starts to make an exaggerated *f* sound and then says, "Father Bear." This is slow processing, but the child is still doing appropriate reading work. She was putting her system to work; it's just not fast and automatic yet. She is going through the process that Singer (1994) describes as "strategic activity":

- Picks up information
- Works on it
- Makes a decision
- Evaluates the response

A child's processing is often slow like this when the strategies in the system are newly acquired, when the network of strategies is under construction. Eventually, with lots of practice time and opportunities to put his system to work, the child's ability to use his system speeds up. The slow processing system gives way to rapid processing (Clay 2001). Look at the same sentence again.

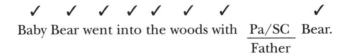

You have probably heard a child fix an error this quickly. This child corrected the mistake in a millisecond, right after he made it. That's fast, automatic processing.

When a reader uses his system of strategies, doing the reading work necessary to solve problems while reading, he is not only reinforcing his system and making it stronger, but also teaching himself new things. In her book *Change over Time in Children's Literacy Development* (2001), Clay explains a study by McNaughton (1985). The researcher showed that students were able to figure out words *while reading* that they had previously missed in isolation. Afterward, the students were able to continue to identify those words in successive encounters whether those words were in context or in isolation. By using their system of strategies they actually taught themselves new words.

When Matching Children to Text Really Matters

A second-grade teacher once told me about a problem she was having with Greg. He refused to read to her (during guided reading or individual reading time) in books appropriate for his reading level. I asked why she thought he was being so resistant. She said, "He walks around carrying Harry Potter [books], even though there is no way he could read that text. He wants to be able to read the kind of book that his older, gifted sister reads." Sometimes children would rather pretend to read than actually read. It's our job to help them experience the intrinsic rewards of reading, find texts that are of interest to them while still being books they can handle, and develop as readers so that they can eventually read their "some-day" books.

I knew Greg was a child who received extra help in first grade. I also knew he had left us in June with a system of strategies in place, and was an on-grade-level reader. This unwillingness to work with the teacher on appropriate-level texts concerned me. I worried about him losing his strategies because of lack of use. The teacher and I decided to involve Greg's mom. She was very supportive of her son's reading development and we wanted to be sure she understood what was going on. Also, Greg was usually very agreeable to things his mom suggested.

During several meetings with the mother, we discussed why Greg needed time in appropriate-level texts. Without practice—using his system of strategies to figure out words and make sense of the texts—he would be in danger of losing that ability. Harry Potter books, for this child, were frustrational-level text, and would not result in his using his system effectively. I suggested that his mom read such chapter books to him at home. She was happy to take on that job.

The classroom teacher and I talked with Greg about *easy, just right,* and *challenge* books and how all children can have time with all three types of books. We also discussed how important it is for students to use the techniques they know for figuring out words; if there were too many words on each page to figure out, then that would be too much work for Greg. We wanted to use books with him that would have just the right amount of work in them. The classroom teacher explained that she would take Greg's interests into consideration and give him some choices in the books they would work on together.

With Mom's urging and the classroom teacher's explanation, Greg became much more relaxed and willing to read books that were more appropriate for him in the classroom. He became more engaged in his guided reading lessons. At night, Mom read a chapter of the Harry Potter books. And I was comfortable with the fact that Greg would continue to put his system to work in texts appropriately matched to his abilities.

Though I don't believe that teachers should overly depend on levels of text for all children, I do think that we have to be sure children are able to read the text with enough ease that they can put their strategies to use. There's a big difference between reading a Henry and Mudge book and a Harry Potter book.

In Brief

- ◊ Encouraging struggling readers to actively initiate strategies and behaviors is an important part of teaching reading and can begin at the very earliest stages.
- ◊ The way we model, support, prompt, reinforce, and praise children can either aid or hinder them in becoming active participants.
- ◊ Explicit demonstrations are necessary to turn passive readers into active ones.
- ◊ At times, our emphasis needs to be on *how to solve* over accuracy in order for struggling readers to take on a strategy or part of a strategy.
- ◊ One goal for readers is to use a balance of meaning, structure, and visual/graphophonic information to solve words. Teachers can encourage balance by prompting for the source of information that the child neglected.
- ◊ Scaffolds can assist students for a time by simplifying the child's role in the task, even while holding the difficulty of the task constant. But scaffolds must eventually be dismantled or let go.
- ◊ Teachers need to provide opportunities for children to practice strategies and put their reading process system to work. The network of strategies that the child is constructing becomes stronger and more efficient through use.
- ◊ The system of strategies becomes self-extending as the child discovers new things for himself while reading.

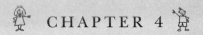

CHAPTER 4

Fluency

When I think of fluency I am reminded of a session I attended at a conference where the participants listened to a tape of an adult reading a children's book in French. The presenter wanted us to listen for all that fluency entails, but not be distracted by the message in English. Having no background in French, I was amazed at what I was able to hear. The grouping of words, the pacing changes the reader used at different points of the story, the intonations, the rise and fall of her voice, the excitement or expression the reader was bringing to bear on the meaning of the text—all this was easily noted even though I understood nothing of what I heard. The presenter's reason for this activity was to help the audience grasp the fact that fluency is not just speed and accuracy, but involves many other aspects.

In order for you to get the same sense of all that fluency encompasses, I've picked some famous lines from books, movies, or speeches. Read them out loud and listen for the many aspects of fluency that you automatically apply because you are a proficient reader.

♦ "It was the best of times. It was the worst of times." (Charles Dickens, *A Tale of Two Cities*)

49

- "Call me Ishmael." (Herman Melville, *Moby Dick*)
- "I have a dream that my four little children will one day live in a nation where they will not be judged by the color of their skin but by the content of their character." (Martin Luther King Jr.)
- "Ask not what your country can do for you; ask what you can do for your country." (John Fitzgerald Kennedy)
- "Are you talking to me?" (Robert De Niro in *Taxi Driver*)
- "Frankly, my dear, I don't give a damn." (Clark Gable in *Gone with the Wind*)

Did you hear how you emphasized certain words, like *best* and *worst* in the first example, or the word *not* in the JFK example? Did you feel yourself grouping particular words together, such as *color of their skin* or *content of their character*? Did your voice rise up a notch at the end of the sentence with a question mark? Did you notice how you separated the words *my dear* with your voice because of the commas?

When children read fluently it isn't any different. A fluent child attends to punctuation to add meaning to the text, phrases words into groups so that they approximate how we would speak those words, speeds up and slows down where appropriate, and uses inflection similar to what is used in oral speech. The opposite of a fluent reader is the monotone or robotic word-by-word reading that some children do. It's easy for a teacher to detect a fluency issue, but understanding what it means for the reader and how one goes about teaching a child to build fluency are more difficult. In this chapter, I take you through the framework with Justin, a beginning struggling reader, who learns to detect for himself when he is sounding fluent and when he is not, and what he learns to do about the latter. The chapter emphasizes the relationship between fluency and comprehension and how teachers can support both. It also discusses how fluency relates to word-solving abilities. And, through examples of teacher/student interactions, it explains the importance of book introductions and book choice in supporting children's fluency.

An Early Reader Who Reads Word by Word

Here's What

Justin was a second-grade boy who came from another district and, according to his teacher, arrived in her classroom with very low literacy skills. He was slow to acquire letters and sound knowledge and, after several months of second grade, was still reading in emergent-level texts. I began to read with Justin to see what I could discover about his difficulties. His fluency issue was easily apparent. His reading was slow and halting. He would look at the first word, call it out, move to the next, call it out, and on it went. This choppy reading was affecting his comprehension, his enjoyment, his motivation to practice reading during individual reading time, and his word-solving abilities.

So What

The classroom teacher, Kara Conques, had also noticed Justin's choppy reading. Since the *so what* phase is a time to reflect and share ideas, we hypothesized about what Justin's lack of fluency might mean. Kara suggested that his choppy reading might have to do with his not recognizing sight vocabulary words quickly enough and wondered whether having him spend time practicing high-frequency words on cards would help. I mentioned that a word-card emphasis could give Justin the impression that reading was more about calling all the words right than about reading for meaning. Though children need to learn to automatically recognize many high-frequency words, they also need to see these words in context. Having a large chunk of time each day for rereading familiar books is a more enjoyable and meaningful way to develop a basic sight vocabulary than isolated flash-card practice.

Kara and I also discussed the possibility, once Justin's fluency increased, that he might be more able to predict unknown words based on the meaning of the sentence. We talked about how we could support the meaning of the story through our book introductions. We thought about book choice and which books would best help Justin develop fluency over the next few days.

Though teaching for fluency can include many aspects, we decided that Justin's most pressing need was associated with phrasing, reading in groups of words. For the immediate teaching that Kara and I would do, we decided to focus our thinking on these questions:

- Is Justin even aware that he sounds choppy?
- Can we help him hear the difference between when he is sounding choppy and when his reading is smooth and well phrased?
- What are the ways we can model and explicitly show Justin what smooth reading is?

- What prompts should we use to remind him to be fluent?
- What are some ways to turn over the responsibility to him for monitoring his own fluency?

As we discussed these questions, we made decisions about our instruction for this student.

Now What

In the teaching examples that follow, you will notice we spent several days on instructing and supporting Justin with fluency teaching.

Day One To begin, Kara observes me working with Justin. He is reading a text he has read several times before, yet he still reads it word by word.

Justin: (*reading in a robotic voice*)
"'Oh, no! It's starting to rain,' said Grandpa.
"'Come on. Hurry!' said Dave.
"'Run! Run to the car,' said Grandpa."

Pat: Justin, I'm going to stop you there for a minute. I noticed you were sounding very choppy on this page. (*I then read a sentence as Justin did, sounding very staccato.*)

Justin: (*laughs and repeats the word* choppy)

Pat: I'd like to show you how to get your reading to sound nice and smooth, more like real talking, and not so choppy. (*I take two index cards and frame a group of words. With the cards framing "It's starting to rain," I read that part to model what I mean.*) Did you hear how I put all those words together? Now you try it.

Justin: (*repeats the phrase, sounding just like I did*) "It's starting to rain."

Pat: Good. Now try putting this part together. (*I frame the words* Come on.)

Justin: "Come on." (*goes back to word-by-word reading*)

Pat: Put it all together, like this: "Come on." Remember it's starting to rain and Dave wants Grandpa to hurry. (*I pull his sweater sleeve and say, "Come on, Justin. Come on." I want him to realize how this phrase sounds when he and I are talking.*) OK. Read it with me from here.

As we continue through the text, I frame some groups of words and Justin practices reading the words together in phrases. Sometimes I have to model the sound of it; sometimes he reads the phrase fluently on his own. On several occasions we stop to talk about what's happening in the story. This brief interaction builds the meaning of the story and directly supports Justin's fluency. It is easier to put groups of words together when you have a stronger sense of what's going on in the book.

Day Two I continue to work with Justin in other familiar books. This time I cover over the words of the book sometimes and have Justin look at me and just repeat a phrase.

Pat: Say it like this, Justin. "Here you are."
Justin: "Here you are."
Pat: Good. It's just like something I would say if you asked me for a pen-cil. Here you are, Justin, here's a pencil for you.

We practice handing each other objects and saying, "Here you are." Saying the phrase without looking at the text helps Justin realize how it sounds in a normal speaking interaction.

I decide not to use the framing cards on this day, but instead push with my thumb behind the words. If he reads a part choppily, I say, "Try it again and put it all together this time." I'm also on the lookout for places where Justin *does* read words together, even if it's just two-word phrases, such as, "said Mom" or "oh, no," so that I can praise him. My teaching for these two days has been focused on getting Justin to hear the difference between choppy and smooth reading. I don't expect him to absorb all there is to learn about fluency in one or two days.

Day Three The next day the teacher reminds Justin about self-monitoring for fluency as he starts to read another familiar book from his book box.

Kara: Remember, Mrs. Johnson has been teaching you how to make your reading sound really smooth. I want you to practice that today. If you hear yourself sounding choppy, go back and put it all together. (*Kara and I agree that we will both use the prompt "put it all together."*)
Justin: (*reads the title and the first page*)
"My New Soccer Uniform. These are my new soccer shoes. They are good for running." (*reads very choppily at first, but then repeats it fluently. Justin then looks up and smiles at the teacher as if wanting approval.*)
Kara: How do you think you sounded? (*She is passing the monitoring job back to him.*)
Justin: Good.
Kara: Great. Then keep going.

Justin: (*begins to reads page 2*) "These are my new soccer shoes." (*Although he reads this sentence fluently, he makes an error. The last word is* shorts, *not* shoes. *He shakes his head when he realizes his error.*)

Kara: Go ahead. You're being a good checker. You know how to fix that.

Because Justin is working so hard to read fluently, some of the other things he's learned to do automatically may take a backseat temporarily. It's our job to remind him of those until he is able to integrate all of these strategic actions together.

Throughout this reading, Kara occasionally has to get the framing cards out, push with her thumb, model with her voice, or discuss the meaning of the page, but overall Justin is beginning to listen to himself to see how he sounds. Over the next few lessons, Kara and I model, support, prompt, or reinforce, continually moving up and down the range of teaching actions, responding to what Justin does or doesn't do.

Follow-up Ideas On subsequent days we tried other techniques. One day I took turns reading alternate pages with Justin. In this way he heard my fluent reading on every other page, and when it was his turn, he tried to imitate my pacing to keep the story moving.

On another day, Kara took a sentence from Justin's story during writing workshop time. After he had written his story in transitional spelling, she wrote it correctly on a sentence strip and cut it into individual words. She then arranged the words in groups on his desk. They practiced reading his sentence with appropriate phrasing:

> My friend Joey   came over to my house yesterday   and we made
> a fort.

This manual grouping of words together (with large spaces between the phrases) really helps make the point of phrasing for readers who do not read fluently. They can actually *see* what we are trying to get them to do with their voice as they read. This is basically the same idea as using the framing cards, but since it is the child's own story, he will be more apt to read it fluently.

Kara and I also picked Justin's new books carefully for the next few days. We wanted lots of opportunities for fluency teaching and reinforcement. Some of these books had phrases that linked easily to his oral language and experiences, such as "What a mess!" or "Oh no!" Other books had characters Justin was familiar with, so we encouraged him to read the dialogue appropriately by saying, "Make it sound just like Mother Monkey talking." Still other books had singsong patterns that made it easy for Justin to group words.

Then What

It was important to continue to observe whether Justin was monitoring his own fluency without reminders from us. As I was taking a running record one day, shortly after we began our work on fluency, I heard him slip back into his old habit of choppy reading on the first few pages. Then, all of a sudden on the fourth page, it was like a lightbulb went on. He must have realized how choppy he was sounding. He read the sentence "They saw some hungry goats" word by word, but then immediately went back and put it together. For the rest of the book he maintained a fluent voice. Of course, I strongly reinforced what he did after the running record was completed.

Some teachers use a simple marking system to note fluency while they are doing running records (see Figure 4–1). To do this, you circle or loop a group of words together that the child read well phrased. Or you put dashes under the check marks when a child reads in a choppy manner. These indicators will help you find the place you want to go back to for a teaching point related to fluency or a place where you want to praise the child's fluent reading.

As children move up in text levels, they learn new strategies and behaviors. Yet we have to be sure they do not lose the ground we've gained on fluency. Though a child's reading of a new text may not be as well phrased in parts, the child who self-monitors for fluency will work at adjusting his pace. He may slow down to solve a problem and then pick up the pace again when the problem is solved. Or he may reread a sentence or part of

Figure 4–1
Running Record
Fluency Marks

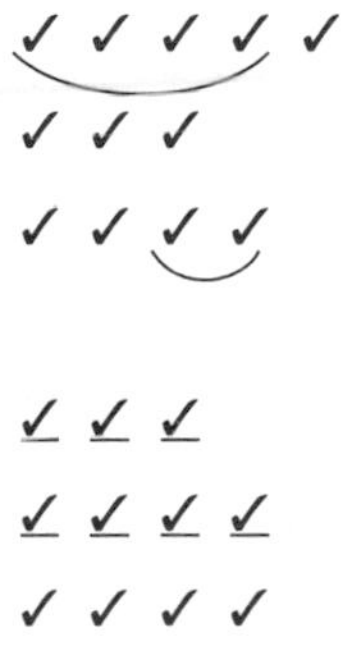

✓ ✓ ✓ ✓ ✓	Use a looping mark to indicate a
✓ ✓ ✓	group of words or a sentence that
✓ ✓ ✓ ✓	the child read well phrased.
✓ ✓ ✓	Put dashes under the check marks to
✓ ✓ ✓ ✓	indicate where the child was reading
✓ ✓ ✓ ✓	in a word-by-word manner.

a sentence if he realized it wasn't well phrased. At times, we may find it necessary to return to some of the modeling or prompting for fluency when the child encounters new difficulties in higher-level texts, as in some of the examples that follow.

How Fluency Supports a Child's Word-Solving Abilities

One of the questions Kara and I wondered about early on was, "Is there a relationship between Justin's ability to figure out new words and his fluency issue?" When a child comes to an unknown word, he needs to use the visual information (the letters and his phonics knowledge) along with the meaning (the context of what comes before the unknown word in the sentence or story) and the structural information (what the child knows about oral language from speaking it). By holding the meaning in his head, the child is better able to predict the unknown word. A fluent reader can predict the unknown word in this example: "I ran out of vanilla extract so I needed to buy some at the _____." The fluent reader would automatically know (based on meaning and structural information) that the missing word could be *store, supermarket, Food Lion,* or any other synonym for *grocery store.*

A child who is not fluent, who reads by considering each word as a separate entity, is more apt to lose the sense of story or meaning of the sentence. Thus, he loses a source of information that could contribute to solving the word and often resorts to the isolated task of sounding it out. On the other hand, an increase in fluency supports the meaning of the text, thereby helping the child better predict unknown words. The more attuned to his fluency Justin became, the more success he had with figuring out unknowns. His newfound ability—to adjust his pacing, to group words together, to attempt to make his voice sound like the characters— helped him maintain a story line. When he came across a tricky word, he would more often than not use the meaning along with the structural and visual information to solve it. This balance of using all sources of information is a goal for every beginning reader.

Book Introductions That Support Fluent Reading

Carefully planned book introductions can support children's fluency as they problem-solve their way through a new text. Marie Clay reminds us of how important these introductions to text are:

As the child approaches a new text he is entitled to an introduction so that when he reads, the gist of the whole or partly revealed story can provide some guide for a fluent reading. He will understand what he reads if it refers to things he knows about, or has read about previously, so that he is familiar with the topic, the vocabulary or the story itself. (1991, p. 335)

When children know a little bit about the story before reading it, they are more likely to use meaningful information as they read. A book introduction at the start of a guided reading lesson often begins with a teacher giving the title of the book, the author, and a brief summary (see Chapter 7 for more information on book introductions). Then the teacher may ask a question to stimulate conversation among the students. Listen in as Sabrina Shea sets the scene for the book *A Tree Horse* with a group of first-grade students.

Sabrina: This book is called *A Tree Horse*. It's about some children who really want a horse, but their parents say they can't have one. So, you know what they do? They make a pretend horse, a tree horse.

Izzy: (*looking at the picture on the cover*) Yeah, they're making believe it's a horse. They got a big branch.

Sabrina: Have you ever wanted something really badly and your parents said you can't have it?

Paul: I wanted a cat but my mom just got a bird.

Maeve: I wanted a dog, but my mom said, "Not right now."

Sabrina: That's just what these parents said: "Not right now. You can't have a horse now." So let's see how the kids made that tree horse. (*She turns to a picture of the tree horse in the middle of the book. The students continue to chat about all the things the kids needed to make the tree horse.*)

Sabrina has carefully planted a sense of this story in the children's heads. She lets the children connect the experience with their own. The conversation surrounding the picture helps build background knowledge for this story as the children talk about the blanket, the rope, and the branch. What Sabrina is doing is twofold. First, she brings some of the vocabulary to the forefront by encouraging conversation rather than drilling on the words in isolation. Second, she models how looking at the pictures and thinking about what we know before reading will help us. Fortified with the meaning of the story, the children are now ready to read the text on their own.

Sometimes, even after a strong book introduction, a child still reads word by word. That's the time to use some of the other techniques mentioned in Justin's story: framing groups of words, pushing with your thumb behind the words, modeling with your voice, pointing out quotation marks where the character is talking, finding a group of words that the child read well phrased to use as a model, or stopping to support the child's comprehension of the text.

One day I ran into some trouble as I read with Eliana, a second-grade English language learner (ELL). The emergent book I chose had a pattern that went something like this:

Come to my backyard.
You can see . . .

On each page the opening sentence was repeated followed by different things the little girl was showing us in her backyard. Each item—ladybugs, flowers, and other objects—was supported by the pictures. My introduction summary went something like this: "We are going to read a book about a little girl who wants us to see all the different things she has in her yard. What do you think we might see in her backyard?" Eliana and I then talked as we examined some of the pictures together. However, when Eliana began to read, she read "*Comes* to my backyard" (very word by word; misreading the word *come*). Though I corrected her two times, she continued to say *comes* for *come*. I found this unusual because it is much more typical for an ELL to leave off the *s* ending than to add one. I tried showing her the difference between the two words visually on a whiteboard, saying, "You see, Eliana, one has an *s* on the end and the other doesn't." By the fourth page I finally figured out what was happening. I could hear her under her breath saying, "Here comes" before she started each page. I realized that Eliana was using a sentence from another book she had read ("Here comes the red wagon. Here comes the blue wagon.") to help her with the word *come*. Later, feeling very unsuccessful with this teacher/child interaction, I reflected on what might have gone wrong and how I could have supported her fluency better.

Most English language learners speak in present tense or present progressive tense (such as, "I am coming" or "He is sitting") before past, future, or other verb structures (Cappellini 2005). This phrase "Come to my backyard" is imperative, the subject "you" being understood. I realized what an awkward and unfamiliar structure this is for an ELL. Though my book introduction prepared her for some of the things in the backyard, it didn't help her with the novel language structure used in this text on every page. I could have practiced this phrase with the child ahead of time, letting her say it a few times to get the feel of it. I could also have elaborated on the meaning of the phrase by using an example outside the text. The next day I went back and tried again.

Pat: This girl in the picture is inviting us to come to her backyard. On every page she says to us, "Come to my backyard." Say that for me. Come to my backyard. (*I am not showing her the text at this point.*)

Eliana: Come to my backyard. (*I ask her to repeat it two more times.*)

Pat: It's just like if I invited you to come to my house and see some things, I might say, "Come to my house. You can see my dog. Come to my house. You can see my ping-pong table." What if I came to your house? What might I see?

Eliana: My mom . . . and my little brother. (*I then encouraged her to say her own examples with the book pattern: "Come to my house. You can see my baby brother. Come to my house. You can see my mom."*)

This experience with Eliana helped me realize the importance of explaining the meaning of a phrase not only as it relates to the context of the story, but also with another example connecting to the child's own life. Practicing that phrase (both with the backyard example and with her home example) readied Eliana to read that sentence fluently on her own. Teachers should keep this in mind when working with ELLs (see also Chapter 7).

The real lesson here is that you can always go back to adjust your teaching. I realized I hadn't built enough support for the language structure into my book introduction. Sometimes the fluency problem is deeper than what it appears to be on the surface. In this case, it wasn't Eliana's misreading of the word *comes* for *come* as much as it was the awkwardness of the whole phrase "Come to my backyard" that was causing her choppy reading.

Book Choice and Fluency

One of the best ways a teacher can support a struggling reader who is working on fluency is to choose books carefully. A child needs some books in his basket or book box that he can read easily. Time for familiar reading each day will provide the child with opportunities to practice reading fluently. Each child needs to know what it feels like to be a fluent reader. Juliza's favorite book is *Lazy Mary,* with the chorus, "Lazy Mary, will you get up? Will you, will you, will you get up? Lazy Mary, will you get up? Will you get up today?" Oftentimes, I use that book as a way for her to gauge her own fluency. I say, "Try to make this one sound as smooth as when you are reading *Lazy Mary.*"

We all know how young children love to join in on the refrains in familiar Big Books, like, "Run, run, as fast as you can. You can't catch me. I'm the Gingerbread Man." Teachers can use shared reading experiences with Big Books or poems on charts to talk to children about reading groups of words together. In *Shared Reading for Today's Classroom* (2005) Carleen Payne gives various ideas of how to use Big Books to model, teach, and practice fluent reading with young children. Other ideas in her book include fluency activities for literacy centers, how to create Readers Theater scripts from familiar stories, and ways to reproduce familiar stories, songs, or poems to use with a take-home reading program.

In Jodi Maher's first-grade room, children love Mem Fox's books. As you pass their room during shared reading, you can hear them reading with great expression. They love exclaiming words, such as, "Good grief!" or "Well, well!" as they enjoy Mem Fox's repeated, singsong phrasing and delightful story lines.

Jodi: How did you know how to read this part so well? (*points to the line "'Good grief!' said the goose."*)
Lindsey: I was sounding like the goose.
Conner: And I saw the exciting mark.

Jodi is choosing Big Books that support fluency teaching during shared reading for the whole class. She knows, however, that some children will need more of a focus on fluency than others, so for guided reading with small groups, she chooses sets of books for these readers that have singsong patterns or repetitive refrains. These books are not only fun to read, but beg to be read fluently. The list on the next page contains a few possible titles.

Carol Felderman, a second-grade teacher, noticed Gary's choppy reading and began to try some of the suggestions I had shared with her. She was having trouble, though, finding just the right book that Gary would be willing to practice over time. Although he enjoyed and understood the books she gave him in guided reading and was beginning to improve his fluency, he rarely reread them during individual reading time. Carol knew

Books with singsong patterns or repetitive refrains:

Oh, Jump in a Sack, by Joy Cowley. The Wright Group. 1998.

Cinderella Dressed in Yellow, by Rozanne Lanczak Williams. Creative Teaching Press. 1995.

There's a Monster in the Tree, by Rozanne Lanczak Williams. Creative Teaching Press. 1995.

Lazy Mary, by June Melser. The Wright Group. 1998.

The Gumby Shop, by Joy Cowley. Rigby. 1988.

Who Took the Cookies from the Cookie Jar?, by Rozanne Lanczak Williams. Creative Teaching Press. 1995.

More Spaghetti, I Say!, by Ruth Golden Gelman. Scholastic. 1992.

I Went Walking, by Sue Williams. Harcourt Children's Books. 1989.

Go, Dog, Go!, by P. D. Eastman. Random House. 1961.

that the familiar practice time was crucial for Gary to build fluency. I located a copy of Joy Cowley's *The Gumby Shop.* This rhyming, rhythmic book is about the weird items you can buy at the Gumby Shop—from "a bear with electric hair" to "a bed made out of bread." The humor appealed to Gary. After reading it together, I suggested that he read it to three of his friends during buddy reading time, since it was so crazy and he read it so well. He left full of excitement that he had a funny book to share with his friends.

Finding books that interest a child so that he will want to reread is not always easy. Other techniques are sometimes needed to keep children like Gary on task during individual reading time. One thing Carol found useful was to let Gary work with a tape recorder once in a while. He would tape himself reading a book, listen to his fluency, then try reading the book again to see if he could sound better. The challenge of trying to sound a little bit more phrased and fluent on the next try kept him engaged and on task.

Intonation and Fluency

Intonation is the rise and fall of our voice at appropriate times or the emphasis we place on one or several words in a sentence. Sometimes the meaning of a sentence requires a certain intonation in order to be understood. For example, try reading these sentences:

"My brother won't help my mom with the baby," said Kayla, "so I do."
"My sister won't help my mom set the table," said Kayla, "so I do."

Did you notice how you read the words *so I do*? You probably stressed the word *I*. The way that particular sentence is read contributes heavily to its meaning. Kayla is thinking, "My brother or sister won't do it, so *I* have to." A student who reads that sentence in a monotone, word-by-word manner may miss the meaning of the sentence even though he read it with 100 percent accuracy. A teacher needs to stop a child in order to help with intonation if she feels it's affecting the child's comprehension. We should especially tune our ears to English language learners when intonation seems to be causing a comprehension problem.

It is especially exciting to see a child figure out the right intonation without support from a teacher. I remember Ibrahim, who read the line "Well done!" in a book (a father was congratulating his son for rescuing a duckling). At first, Ibrahim just read the words choppily and without any expression. He had a puzzled look on his face, as if meaning had just broken down for him. He repeated the words two or three times and then it finally hit him. Without my intervening, he read, "Well done!" with appropriate expression. I asked, "Why do you think the dad said that?" And he answered, "Because his father is saying he did a good job." It was through the proper intonation that Ibrahim gained the meaning of that phrase. What is wonderful about this example is that Ibrahim was not satisfied with just reading the words correctly. He was self-monitoring for meaning enough to know that something didn't make sense to him and he kept trying until it did. On his fourth try he was able to capture the meaning by changing his intonation.

Punctuation and Fluency

Learning to read the punctuation can start very early with beginning readers and might need to be reemphasized with struggling readers in a small group or one-on-one. Quotation marks, question marks, and exclamation points are some of the first marks of punctuation, besides the period, that children can learn to notice and respond to as readers. During shared reading a teacher can help students notice quotation marks (perhaps calling them "talking marks") as she models changing her voice to emphasize the emotion of the character or to show a character asking a question or speaking loudly. Beginning readers can also learn that the voice we use when we are saying the words that the character says out loud is different from the voice we use for the speaker tag ("asked Mama Bear"). Speaker tags are read with our narrator voice: "Why do you think there is a monster under your bed?" asked Mama Bear.

After modeling in shared reading what the different marks of punctuation indicate for the voice of the reader, children can be reminded with prompts during guided reading.

Teacher: (*to a child who just read in a monotone voice*) You read those words correctly, Emma, but I want to hear you sound like Baby Bear might sound.

Emma: (*tries again, this time with better expression*) "'Help! I don't know my way home!' said Baby Bear."

Teacher: That's it. How do you think Baby Bear is feeling in this part of the story?

Emma: Scared.

Teacher: You're right. So make it sound like he's scared when you read that part from now on.

Teacher: (*continues*) Show me where Baby Bear started talking.

Emma: (*points to the beginning quotation marks*)

Teacher: Now show me where he finished talking. Good. Those talking marks are going to help you decide when to make your voice sound like the character of Baby Bear.

We need to teach explicitly to help certain children realize specifically which part the character is saying out loud. You may have to write a sentence from the book on a sentence strip, cut up the words, and have the child help you place the quotation marks in the appropriate place. This manual activity will help the child better understand how quotation marks are sending a message to the reader. When I did this with second grader Owen recently, he said, "I never saw those things before." And yet I am sure that his kindergarten and first-grade teachers had done whole-class activities to help students notice and learn the purpose of quotation marks. Struggling readers often need a second dose of a lesson, and a third, and a fourth.

As I was packing up my things after meeting with Owen, he said, "What's that for?" pointing to a special marker I had. After answering his question I quickly wrote, "'What's that for?' asked Owen" on a sentence strip and cut it up. He smiled as he reconstructed the sentence and placed the quotation marks around the correct part, proud that those were his exact words.

Common Confusers

In certain texts, even the simple use of a comma, a dash, or an ellipsis can cause confusion for some children. This section looks at examples that might confuse a struggling reader and cause a fluency problem.

Direct Address

"Sara, it's lunch time," said Mom.
"Father Mouse, is Baby Mouse with you?" asked Mother Mouse.

Tell students explicitly what's happening. For example, "Mom is talking to Sara here. She's calling to her, telling her it's time for lunch. Whenever a writer wants to show us that a character is talking to someone, he uses a comma after the person's name." You can even write a quick sentence together with the child to make the point more personal. "Nataly, do you like to swim?" Showing the reciprocity between reading and writing is always beneficial.

Added Clause   Sometimes when a phrase is added to the end of the sentence, the child misreads it: "We waited for the seed to grow day after day." It's not unusual to hear a student read that extra clause as if it starts a new sentence, sounding like this, "We waited for the seed to grow. Day after day . . ." We have to stop a child who misreads the punctuation and explicitly teach him or her how the punctuation can help.

Teacher: Let's try that again. Show me where the period is.
Child: (*indicates the period*)
Teacher: OK. That means the end of the sentence, doesn't it? So we have to keep reading until we get to the end of the sentence. Listen to me read it and then you can try it.

Speaker Tag Placed Before the Dialogue   The first time a child comes across a speaker tag *before* the quotation can cause confusion, as in this example:

Squirrel said to the rabbit,
"Please can you help me find some nuts?"

A struggling reader may need help learning how to decide which speaker tag goes with which quote and how a reader's voice sounds in that instance.

Ellipses or Dashes   Some texts use ellipsis points on one page for surprise purposes or for the reader to anticipate what's coming on the next page.

And for her birthday she got a great big . . .
When I grow up I want to be a . . .

Teachers can explain what an ellipsis mark is for and then model what it means for the voice of a reader. Try telling the child, "These three dots mean the sentence isn't finished yet; let your voice trail off like this as you turn the page." Then demonstrate how it should be read. "Your voice is showing that there's still more to come."

Other books have sentences containing a dash, which some children need to learn how to read appropriately:

Look—a tugboat!

Modeling how to make a small pause at a dash is usually all that's needed.

A *Clause Separated by Commas* In nonfiction text it is very common to see important vocabulary words in bold print. Children usually pick up quite easily on the fact that this indicates a key word. What some don't realize, though, is that the definition for that boldfaced word is often right there in the same sentence. Examples of this would be:

Many bears **hibernate,** or go into a sleeplike state, in caves or dens.
Snakes are reptiles. They have scaly skin, forked tongues, and are **verte-brates,** that is, have backbones.

What is obvious to us is not always obvious to struggling readers. I once had a fifth-grade student who was not doing well comprehending her social studies or science texts. I discovered that one of her problems was this exact thing. She was very surprised to learn that the definition for the boldfaced word was right there in the sentence. When I showed her how to look for signal words (Hoyt 2002) such as *is called, that is, or,* or *which means* along with the commas, she was thrilled to be let in on the secret that all the other students seemed to know.

I include these examples from texts to raise teachers' awareness. We all need to take note of the many ways that misunderstanding of a punctuation cue can lead to a fluency (and comprehension) issue with some children. Not reading the punctuation or clauses correctly not only doesn't sound right, but can also contribute to the child's loss of meaning.

Anticipating Novel Punctuation Issues

Teachers can anticipate and allow the children practice time with sentences containing novel punctuation during the book introduction. I watched Carrie Omps begin a guided reading lesson with second graders. The book was about a boy who goes fishing with his dad on weekends. She gave the children the title and a short summary of the book, then asked a question to get the children talking about their experiences or knowledge of fishing. But she didn't end her book introduction there. She had previously noticed that these children often stumbled or became confused when sentences were lengthy and contained several commas. So she added a little practice time to her book intro. A line of the text reads, "So Danny woke up early, and together they went fishing, just like every other weekend."

Carrie: We're going to work on a tricky part before you read this book on your own. In this book, it says, "So Danny woke up early"—say that for me.

Children: "So Danny woke up early . . ."

Carrie: "and together they went fishing . . ." (*holds her palm out toward the children so they know to echo her*)

Children: "and together they went fishing."

Carrie: Now wait, there's more . . . "just like every other weekend."

Children: "just like every other weekend."

Carrie: Say that whole thing with me again. (*They say it again in unison.*)

Carrie: (*handing each child a copy of the book*) Now find that sentence on this page and practice it yourself.

After they practiced, Carrie pointed out the commas and talked about how the commas help a reader decide which parts to read together.

Lengthy sentences containing lots of clauses can stump readers of any age. Students may be able to read all the words, but become confused about the meaning because of the way they misread the punctuation. Take a look at this passage from a fluent-level text:

I am my grandmother's responsibility during weekdays since she doesn't have a job "outside the home." She takes me to see Churchill Downs, where the Kentucky Derby is run, takes me to Frisch's Big Boy drive-in for a secret fish sandwich ("Don't tell Mamaw. She'll claim I ruined your appetite for the nice supper she's making."), takes me to Penney's and buys me new clothes, because she doesn't have time to sew them from scratch herself, since it's too hot in Louisville for what I've brought from Seattle.

If she notices the looks we get from some of the salesladies and waitresses, looks that ask what a normal-looking white lady like my grandmother is doing with a different-colored kid like me, she never once lets on. (Dorris 1999, p. 62)

Think about which students in your class might have trouble reading this page fluently and understanding it. And then think about what you might do to support them.

Teachers can become more sensitive to possible punctuation problems and their effects on fluency. For many struggling readers, learning to read the punctuation correctly can easily be cleared up with appropriate instruction.

Try this with your colleagues at your next grade-level meeting:

- ◆ Bring some books that your students are reading.
- ◆ Take some time to examine them with your colleagues.
- ◆ Look for unusual or novel punctuation that may challenge your students.
- ◆ Brainstorm how you might support your readers who struggle with these issues.

Finger Pointing—A Help or a Hindrance?

In *Teaching for Comprehension in Reading* (2003), Andrea McCarrier brings together the current research in her chapter on fluency. She emphasizes how fluency teaching can take place throughout the day in many different contexts—interactive read-alouds, shared reading, guided reading, and independent mini-lessons. By carrying the thread of your instructional point through many contexts, you will have more chance of reaching all of your students.

McCarrier also answers the question often asked by teachers, "What about finger pointing? Should we encourage it? Is there a time we should discourage it?" With beginning readers we often point to each word in a Big Book. We continue to do this when working with children who do not yet have control over voice/print matching. Eventually, as they gain control, they need to have their eyes do the job that the finger used to do. For a short time before the eyes fully take over, you may actually see a child do some head bobbing, pointing with his nose a bit! McCarrier writes,

> When word-by-word matching is well under control, however, we want the eyes to take over the process. We want readers to begin to combine words into meaningful phrases as their eyes move quickly across them. This is the time to move away from external mediators such as the finger or pointer, which ultimately can interfere with fluency. (p. 155)

McCarrier suggests, at this point, using a sweeping motion with your hand under the words of the enlarged text or pointing only to the beginning of each line.

    Occasionally I come across a child who is still finger pointing long after she needs to be. When I see finger pointing interfering with a child's fluency, so that her reading sounds choppy rather than well phrased, I gently push the hand away from the page and say, "Keep going. I don't think you need your finger anymore. Your eyes can do the job." With other children, I have to remind them that it's OK to use their finger when they are solving a problem, but once the problem is solved the finger should leave the page.

Thinking Aloud About Fluency

Many teachers do not realize just how explicit an explanation some children need. It's not enough to say, "Don't forget to read the punctuation" or "Commas mean slight pauses." Children need clear demonstrations with the teacher thinking aloud about how she decided to read a particular sentence in a particular way. In her fourth-grade class, Stanzi Lowe clearly demonstrated her own thinking with a passage from the book *Wringer* by Jerry Spinelli, which she was reading aloud to her class. For this quick, ten-minute mini-lesson, she put a passage on the overhead for everyone to see. It came from a chapter they had listened to on the previous day.

> But then, come to think of it, he himself could have written many pages about his own pigeon. (And no question now—it was *his*.) He could write about the pigeon tapping on the window every afternoon until he let it in. The pigeon strutting across the sill and onto his bed, then flying from spot to spot in the room, perching

for a moment at every stop, as if to say, *Just making sure everything's as I left it.* (1997, p. 91)

Stanzi began the mini-lesson by telling the students how important it is to watch the punctuation as you read. "The writer gives you hints," she told them, "and those hints help you make decisions about how a passage should be read and that helps you better understand what you are reading." She then walked the students through this example, stopping to think aloud about the commas, the parentheses, and the italicized words. Afterward, she gave the students a copy of a passage from the next chapter that she would be reading that day. The students were to discuss the punctuation cues with a partner and decide together how to read it.

Strickland, Ganske, and Monroe (2002) talk about supporting third-through sixth-grade readers with fluency issues. They offer lots of ideas for practice with fluency, such as: Readers Theater, reading into a tape recorder to practice for a read-aloud performance, preparing a read-aloud book for a younger student, and paired reading experiences. These practice ideas are beneficial for all students, but for a child who has some intense fluency problems, the practice comes *after* the child has been explicitly taught about fluency.

What About Speed?

Recently I've noticed that fluency is frequently equated with speed. I have seen workbooks specifically designed to have children time themselves on passages, practicing over and over to increase their speed. That sort of practice sends a message to children that "proficient readers read fast." Emphasis on speed is misleading, especially in today's competitive video-game society. Children can actually learn to read fast and still not be fluent or understand what they read.

When I interact with a child who interprets fluency to mean speedy, I take time to model the difference between *fast* and *fluent.* I say, "Listen, I can read this slowly and smoothly, like this" (I read something at a moderate pace but well phrased) "or I can read it fast and choppy like this" (then I read the same passage fast, but word by word).

Proficient readers read well paced and well phrased. I try not to use the terms *fast* or *speed* with the children I work with. When teaching for fluency, as with everything else, my main message to children is always: Read to understand, and when meaning breaks down, stop and do something about it.

In Brief

- ◆ Fluency is more than speed and accuracy; it is also pacing, phrasing, reading punctuation cues, expression, and intonation.
- ◆ Children's fluency can be improved with explicit instruction.
- ◆ By talking with colleagues and examining texts together, teachers can raise their own awareness of fluency issues that can affect a child's comprehension.
- ◆ Book introductions play an important role in supporting fluency because they put the meaning of the book in the head of the reader, allowing him to better anticipate the story or the information in the text.
- ◆ Teaching how to read punctuation cues to support meaning construction can be modeled in shared reading with Big Books, with shared demonstrations on the overhead, in guided reading lessons, or one-on-one with students.
- ◆ Careful book choices can support a student's fluency practice.
- ◆ Various techniques, such as framing words, oral modeling, pushing behind the words, or manually separating a sentence into groups of words, help students learn about pacing and phrasing.
- ◆ Rereading familiar text provides opportunities for fluency practice; children need time each day for independent reading.
- ◆ One goal of teaching for fluency is to have the child monitor and repair lack of fluency. A child's reading should have smooth passages, slowing down to solve problems but then regaining fluency after the problem is solved.

CHAPTER 5

Self-Monitoring
for Comprehension

My sixth-grade teacher, Sister Katherine Marie, sat us in rows according to our reading scores on a standardized reading test given the first week of school. Luckily I was a decent reader and therefore claimed the first, second, or third chair of the first row, depending on how I scored on subsequent tests each marking period. Two of my friends occupied the other two seats, and although it didn't seem to matter to us who sat first, second, or third, we all felt that anything lower than that would have been humiliating. I never once gave a thought to what it must feel like to be the last three kids in the last row! The message the teacher sent about *those* children came through loud and clear—they just weren't trying hard enough. And none of us in the first row doubted that that was the truth.

The combination of being one of the best readers in the class and, at the same time, being one of the biggest worriers made for an interesting twist. I was so worried about losing my prized seat in the first row that I panicked when asked to read aloud to the class, a daily occurrence in our social studies, geography, and Bible history books. Round-robin reading occupied half our day. Though I sounded fine to all the listeners, I did not understand one word of what I read! My nervousness won out over my comprehension. Needless to say, that sixth-grade experience taught me many things about what *not* to do as a teacher of reading.

Though I wasn't able to comprehend in that classroom when asked to read aloud, I did have a system in place for comprehending. I took the books home, reread the passages I had missed, and readied myself for tests. Nonetheless, through that experience I know what it feels like to read words and not get anything out of the passage. As adult readers we've all caught ourselves at one time or another getting to the bottom of a page and realizing that our mind was on something other than the text. Since we self-monitor, we know enough to stop and go back in order to recapture the meaning of that page.

There are children, however, who don't stop. They habitually read by merely calling the words. They don't do the thinking that's supposed to accompany the reading of the words, whether they're reading silently or aloud. Some students read right past a difficult word by substituting several sounds in place of a real word, and continuing on. Others put in a real word that might look visually similar to the word in the text, but doesn't make sense, and they, too, keep right on going. Still others can read all the words correctly and yet aren't able to attach meaning to what they just read. All these children are struggling with reading; they're not self-monitoring for understanding. They don't stop when meaning breaks down and they do nothing to fix up their errors or confusions because they have no system in place to monitor their comprehension, nor do they have access to strategies that might help them comprehend.

This chapter looks first at the framework with Sam, a fifth-grade boy who had limited comprehension abilities, then presents several lessons on teaching students self-monitoring and comprehension strategies, and finally, gives suggestions for guiding older readers who struggle with comprehension through a novel unit.

An Upper-Grade Student Who Doesn't Self-Monitor for Comprehension

Here's What

If you walked into Sam's fifth-grade classroom you would hardly notice him. He's small and extremely soft-spoken, and constantly works hard at doing exactly what he is supposed to be doing. During individualized reading time each day, you can see Sam with his book box, filled mostly with nonfiction animal books. He quietly takes out a book and proceeds to read, careful not to disturb others around him or bring any attention to himself. It took an excellent teacher, Sarah VanderZanden, who meets regularly with her students for individual reading conferences, to recognize Sam as a struggling reader. In another classroom he may have gone unnoticed. Since I was working periodically in her classroom, Sarah asked me to take a look at this student, so that we could share our insights and make appropriate plans for helping him. Together we came up with the following list:

- He has a fairly large sight vocabulary.
- He tends to read quickly, but not necessarily with proper phrasing.
- He chooses books that are too difficult for him.
- Though his eyes seem to travel across every word and he appears to be diligently reading, he is not getting much meaning out of what he reads.
- He can't retell or share information about most of what he's read.
- He rarely infers or makes any connections from his reading to his life.
- He has a deep interest in facts about animals, but gets more of his knowledge from Discovery Channel TV than from books.
- Some of the time he reads the punctuation correctly, but more than half the time he reads past the punctuation cues without the proper intonation or expression.
- He doesn't seem to be bothered by the fact that he is not gaining information or enjoying what he is reading.

So What

During the reflective stage, Sarah and I discussed what we thought was going on with Sam. We believed that he had the wrong impression of what reading was all about. He seemed to think that his job as a reader was to keep calling the words as best he could, to give the appearance of a competent reader, and not ask for help or appear confused. He did not see reading as a source of pleasure; as a way to gain information; or as containing ideas that could make you wonder, laugh, cry, or respond in any number of ways. He didn't seem to be getting any intrinsic rewards from reading. Sam's purpose for reading—to please the teacher by "looking like a reader"—might be motivation enough for him in elementary school, but we worried that someday, perhaps next year when he started middle school, it would not sustain him and he would give up. We wanted to be sure Sam left Sarah's classroom with a better sense of the rewards of read-ing, so we made that our overarching goal.

We also felt that Sam needed help learning how to choose books that were appropriate for him. Sarah had already done several whole-class les-sons teaching students about how to differentiate among *easy, just right,* and *challenging* texts at the beginning of the school year, but this student needed some one-on-one assistance with book choice in the school library and in the classroom.

Another of Sam's issues, and by far the most debilitating, was his lack of self-monitoring for comprehension. We needed to address this head-on. He first needed to recognize when he comprehended and when he didn't in order to stop himself whenever meaning broke down. After that, we could support the development of comprehension strategies, such as mak-ing connections, questioning, visualizing, and inferring, to help him stay engaged with text. Meaning, according to Louise Rosenblatt (1994), is the result of the interaction between the reader and the text, and as far as we could tell Sam did not interact much with the information in texts.

By prioritizing our teaching decisions we came up with the following ideas:

- Develop a lesson for the whole class about what comprehension is, what it feels like, and how to monitor for it. Then use that anchor les-son to work with Sam one-on-one.
- Support Sam with choosing books that are *just right* for him, texts on his instructional level.
- Teach whole-class lessons on inferring the meanings of words by using context clues. Support Sam as he implements this new learning.
- Model several ways to code text or use a response log to support Sam's thinking as he reads.
- Work on ways to improve Sam's fluency, particularly his problems with reading the punctuation cues.
- Begin a book club group with Sam as one of the members. Model, scaf-fold, prompt, and reinforce students in various comprehension strate-gies using the book group text. *The Tiger Rising* by Kate DiCamillo was the novel chosen for this book club.
- Use the book club experience—negotiating the meaning of the text with peers, searching together for evidence of our ideas and conclu-sions, experiencing the suspense and excitement of a good book, shar-ing our predictions and responses—to bring Sam closer to the intrin-sic rewards that reading can bring to a reader.

Now What

The *now what* stage for this student was a long-term undertaking. Lack of comprehension is the biggest of all stumbling blocks. The one gift Sarah and I gave ourselves (and Sam for that matter) was time. We knew that we would be working with Sam on these issues for most of his fifth-grade year. There is no magic three-lesson formula that solves a problem such as this. Sam had spent several years developing the habit of reading words without attending to meaning. It was going to take time to support his construction of a system that recognized a lack of comprehension and offered the means by which to fix it. Cris Tovani describes a similar student: "He expects meaning to arrive immediately after he reads the words. He doesn't know good readers construct meaning" (2000, p. 16). Our main focus would be to teach Sam ways to construct the meaning of text *as* he read the words, but first we had to raise his awareness level so he'd monitor for when he comprehended and when he didn't.

Week One During the first week, Sarah taught a lesson with the whole class on what the word *comprehension* entails and whose job it is to check on understanding (see also the mini-lesson that follows the framework). Her goal for the lesson was to have the students understand that when meaning breaks down for them, it is their job to stop and do something about it. I followed up by meeting with Sam one-on-one to reinforce what he learned in that anchor lesson. I used some short passages from a book on wolves, to give him some practice in stopping as soon as meaning is lost.

Pat: Ms. VanderZanden told me she taught a lesson on comprehension this morning. Do you remember what she said about that?

Sam: I'm not sure.

Pat: Do you know what comprehension is?

Sam: I think it means you have to understand what you read.

Pat: That's right. And the reader, me or you or anyone, has to keep checking on that. It's like your brain keeps asking you, "How am I doing? Do I understand this part?" Sam, what if your brain says, "Uh-oh, I'm getting confused here"? What should you do?

Sam: Stop reading?

Pat: That's exactly right. First you have to stop yourself when you don't know a word, when something you read didn't sound quite right to you, or when you just don't get what's happening in the book. That's what we're going to practice doing today—stopping yourself and admitting you are confused when the words aren't making any sense to you.

As we read and discussed the passages about how wolves live, hunt, and raise their young, I encouraged Sam to stop himself when he didn't know a word, rather than making a few sounds or putting in a nonmeaningful word as he normally would. He did this a few times on his own. At other times, I had to stop him when he tried to speed by, misreading a word or phrase. I would say, "Sam, you just read this [then I'd reread the sentence including his error]—does that make sense to you?" I was supporting him by modeling the monitoring that he should have been doing in his head. Eventually that role of monitoring would be turned over to him, but for now I was acting as the voice in his head.

After a few pages I wanted Sam to expand his monitoring beyond merely stopping at unknown words. I also wanted him to know if he thought he understood whole sections or not. So I asked him to stop after each paragraph. He could do one of two things at that point: (1) he could tell me in his own words what he learned about wolves in that section, or (2) he could say he didn't understand that part. Either way, I accepted his response. I wanted him to know there was no penalty for not understanding. I narrowed my focus to the self-monitoring aspect of reading; I was not yet concerned if Sam knew ways to fix up his confusions. We were working only on a sense of becoming *the checker* of your own reading. Sarah and I kept this as our focus point whenever we had opportunities to read with Sam that first week.

Sarah also retaught her lesson on choosing appropriate books, working with Sam and one other student, Carl. This involved staying with the children as they picked a few books off the shelf in the classroom. The students would read the first page or two and decide if they understood all of it, most of it, or hardly any of it. Sarah was right there with them, guiding their decisions on whether the book was *easy* for them (meaning they read it fluently, understood it all, and had no trouble solving the words), *just right* (they understood most of it, even though they had to stop and figure out a few words, or had to reread a few times), or *challenging* for them (the book seemed too hard to read fluently and they didn't understand what the text was about).

In Sarah's room, students are encouraged to spend most of their time in their *just right* books during individualized reading time each day. They can keep a *challenge* book in their book box also, as long as they recognize it as such. There may be other times of the day when a student will have a few minutes to browse through his challenge book. Many students do this to enjoy the pictures of the animal nonfiction books in the room. Even when they are not able to read that book cover to cover, students can often pick up information from the picture captions, graphs, or diagrams. Students often pick their challenge book to use during buddy reading time, especially if the buddy is a stronger reader and can read some interesting parts to the struggling reader.

Likewise, students are also allowed to keep an *easy* book, one they just enjoy rereading even though it presents no challenges. The easy, smooth way they are able to read this text can provide fluency practice and relaxed enjoyment.

Doing the book choice activity was more difficult for Sam than for Carl. Carl had a slightly better handle on when he comprehended and when he didn't, so the process of choosing books went smoothly for him. Sam, on the other hand, had not had a lot of experience with the feel of "when I'm comprehending and when I'm not." Therefore, he kept judging the books based solely on whether he knew the words. Sarah played a more involved role in helping Sam choose his books. She also repeated this same kind of attention with him the next time the class went to the library to select books.

When I read with Sam later that week, he was excited to show me a book about money and another on finding a man buried in the ice on Mt. Everest that he had chosen from the library. He read parts of each book to me and was able to talk about them, laugh, explain the humor in the money book, and make solid predictions in the other one. Afterward, our conversation went something like this:

Pat: How did you feel about what you read today?

Sam: I like both these books. The money one is my favorite.

Pat: Did you feel you comprehended what you read today?

Sam: Yes, these books are kind of easy for me.

Pat: I know you knew a lot of the words in these books, Sam, but I want to tell you what I liked that you did today. It was something I've never seen you do before.

Sam: What?

Pat: Over here when you read, "They must be penny-pinchers," you asked me what *penny-pinchers* meant. That showed me you were thinking about the words in the book and checking on yourself. When you didn't know what that phrase meant, you stopped and asked me about it. Remember when Ms. VanderZanden talked to the class the other day, saying, "If you don't understand something, you need to stop yourself, or it could only get worse"? (*He nods.*) Well, it seems to me that you're starting to do just that. Great job today! (*I've taken some time here to hook what Sam was beginning to do—monitoring his understanding—to the anchor lesson the teacher taught the whole class a few days prior.*)

Sam was enjoying reading because the books were no longer too hard for him to comprehend. When a child is constantly reading at a comprehension frustration level, he doesn't enjoy what he is doing. Sam could read the words of harder texts, but he wasn't able to comprehend at that level. He needed help picking books based on his comprehension, rather than just choosing books based on how many words he could call.

Week Two   The second week I taught a whole-class lesson on context clues (a detailed mini-lesson can be found later in the chapter). The classroom teacher and I felt there were enough students in the room, in addition to Sam, who would benefit from learning how to figure out the meanings of words from the context of the sentence. I taught the students by first modeling my thinking while I figured out a difficult vocabulary word, then we did several words together as a class, and finally the students worked on a few examples with partners. All the words used in the lesson came from a book I read aloud to the class. As part of the lesson, the class collaboratively created a chart that documented the process of using context clues. After the anchor lesson, both Sarah and I held Sam accountable for using the class chart. The chart outlined a procedure that Sam could follow when he was confronted with difficult vocabulary. Although he didn't always stop himself, we supported him with prompts ("You need to go back and check on something that wasn't quite right in that sentence" or "How can you help yourself figure out that hard word?"), which encouraged his self-monitoring of unfamiliar vocabulary words. With time and practice, we knew Sam would eventually initiate the use of context clues more consistently on his own.

Weeks Three and Four   Since Sam did not always read the punctuation correctly, Sarah and I spent some time focusing on this issue. We used many of the ideas for fluency from Chapter 4.

During these weeks, Sarah and I also introduced several techniques to support Sam as he was learning to better monitor his comprehension and construct meaning. We used *highlighting text* with markers (Tovani 2000) to indicate when he understood and when he didn't. We used *coding text* with symbols (Harvey and Goudvis 2000) to mark places when he was confused or when he found important or surprising information. Giving students a way to code or mark text nudges them to do the necessary thinking while reading. We also taught ways to stop and *paraphrase information* after reading sections of text. And we used the *patterned sentence* "I think (this) because (this)" (Fay and Whaley 2004) as a way for him to respond in his response log. This helped him find evidence in the text for his conclusions.

Weeks Five Through Eight: Sam as a Member of a Novel Unit Group During the next few weeks we formed a book group with Sam and several students, all of whom had some comprehension problems. As part of the book group, we modeled and supported the students using several comprehension strategies. We chose *The Tiger Rising* (2001) by Kate DiCamillo for a variety of reasons. The teacher had recently read aloud *Because of Winn-Dixie* by the same author. The students had all enjoyed that book and were now familiar with the author's style of writing. The two books lend themselves well to making text-to-text connections. The chapters in *The Tiger Rising* are short, which keeps struggling readers from feeling overwhelmed by assignments. The book also has many places where students need to infer beyond the literal level in order to understand what's going on.

The story has two main characters, Rob and Sistine, classmates who are captivated by a tiger that Rob recently found in the woods, locked in a cage. Rob, who lives with his dad in a run-down motel, is troubled by the death of his mom, but holds all his feelings inside of him. He's extremely shy and is continually plagued by the antics of the bullies in school. Sistine, a child of a troubled marriage, recently arrived from another state. She wears her anger for everyone to see, often starting fights at school. She is furious that her mom has taken her to such a ridiculous town and holds onto the hope that her dad will come rescue her.

The story has all the ingredients of a suspenseful adventure, complete with a strong friendship, a bit of tragedy, and young characters who grow up a bit as a result of challenging events and circumstances. It has opportunities for teaching many of the comprehension strategies that this group of students needed experience with. A few examples follow:

1. *Visualizing and inferring.* Before reading Chapters 1 through 4, we told the students that an author often begins a book by letting you know where and when it's taking place (setting) and introduces you to the characters. We asked students to visualize the place and the characters

as they read these chapters and to make a few sketches. We talked about the words in the text that helped them decide on their mental images. Our discussion of these chapters also centered on the personality traits of the characters we met so far and some predictions about how they might behave in the book. We worked on teaching the children how to support their conclusions and predictions with evidence from the text. Possible teacher talk:

"Which words or phrases helped you draw that picture?"
"How do you know that _____?"
"Show a part in the book that made you think that."

2. *Self-monitoring for setting changes.* There are many times in the text when Rob flashes back to a scene when his mother was still alive. The author does this subtly, and the readers needed support in recognizing the signs of when the action was present day and when it was part of a flashback. By examining two flashbacks carefully with the children when they occurred early in the book, the students became more astute at recognizing when a flashback occurred at other points in the novel. Possible teacher talk:

    "Show me where the flashback started."
    "Show me where it ended."
    "What words gave you a hint that Rob was reminiscing?"

3. *Comprehending character development.* Since we had spent time discussing characters at the start of the book, we were able to turn more responsibility over to the students when a new character appeared in the middle of the text. Possible teacher talk:

    "Readers, remember how we inferred so many things about the characters Rob, Sistine, Norton and Billy, and Rob's dad by paying attention to what they said and did? That's how authors develop their characters. Well, in this next chapter, you are going to meet a new character, Willie May. Find out as much as you can about who she is and what she's like by paying attention to what she does and says as you read today."

4. *Inferring.* There were many opportunities with this text to support the children as they inferred what the character or author meant by cer-

tain statements. For example, we discussed when Willie May says, "You got to let that sadness rise on up" (p. 37) or when the author writes, "The word was as sweet as forbidden candy on his tongue" (p. 60).

5. *Point of view.* By the middle of the text four characters (Rob, Sistine, Beauchamp, and Willie May) knew of the existence of the tiger. The classroom teacher and I decided to work on perspectives; that is, how each of the four characters viewed the tiger and what they thought should be done with it. This helped students understand how certain events or issues in a text can be viewed differently by various characters. Possible teacher talk:

"Did Rob agree with Sistine about setting the tiger free?"
"Mr. Beauchamp says he wants to make money off the tiger. How might he do that?"
"Which character's perspective would you take if you were there with them and had to make a decision about the tiger?"

6. *Picking out important parts.* There are no chapter titles in this text, only numbers. Therefore, we asked the children to create titles for some chapters. By doing so they had to figure out the main idea or most important event in that chapter in order to create a title that reflected that, but didn't give away too much.

7. *Responding to the text.* We used a variety of ways to respond in a response log; for example, T-charts. On the left side of the T-chart, children filled in three things they learned in the chapter. On the right side, they wrote "what I think about that." This technique served as a conversation starter when students came back together to discuss the reading.

Sam's tendency to be one of the quieter ones in the group meant he didn't readily volunteer his feelings or responses to the events in the novel. Though this made it difficult for us to gauge his comprehension, we never gave up; we just adjusted our teaching. We learned that he always did better when there was a specific purpose set. For example, if we just asked him to read the chapter and bring back his thoughts to the group, he wouldn't contribute much. But if we said, "Find out how the friendship develops between the two main characters in this chapter," he participated much more. Likewise, if we charted the students' questions before reading a specific chapter, Sam's level of engagement was higher. He enjoyed reading to find the answers to his and other students' questions.

The experience of reading and discussing a chapter book with friends paid off for this group of struggling readers. A few gained more confidence. I heard Manuel saying to one of the most capable readers in the class, "Ryan, this is a really great book. You might want to read it when I'm done. You can borrow my copy if you want." Another child, Evan, became more confident when inferring and discovering underlying meanings in the text—even though he was the one student who needed a partner to read a lot of the text to him. Carl became the context clues expert. He often picked out the more difficult vocabulary words to bring back to the group and showed them how he figured out what the words might mean. And the book motivated Sam and Maria for future reading. Both asked if there were any more books by this author that they could find in the school library.

Perhaps the most rewarding feedback came when Sarah discovered an entry in Sam's response log one day, long after the novel unit had ended. It read, "I really liked the tiger book. I hope I can find another one just like it. No teacher ever gave me a chapter book before. They always gave me baby books in third and fourth grade." Literacy expert Frank Smith (1994, 1998) says that all children need to feel they are part of the "literacy club." Setting the bar a little bit higher for this struggling reader, but then offering him the supports he needed, was our way of welcoming him into the literacy club.

Then What

As I mentioned earlier, the *now what* phase took place over several months. The observational stage, therefore, paralleled that teaching. Sarah and I regularly took notes on the techniques we used with Sam, assessing which ones were helping his comprehension the most. Our data included anecdotal notes; an assessment sheet when listening to him read orally (see Appendix A); notes on his responses during guided reading or individual conferences; and an examination of the work he did when highlighting, coding text, or responding in his log. We observed which techniques he was becoming more comfortable with and which ones seemed to get in the way of his thinking. When he read aloud to us we looked for instances where he self-monitored, stopping when he lost meaning. We noted times when he self-initiated fix-up strategies and when we had to prompt for their use.

Compared to the September observations, our data by March showed that Sam had made considerable progress in his ability to self-monitor for comprehension, and in building a system for constructing meaning as he read. He had learned several ways to help himself think about his reading—using context clues; marking text with connections, questions, or important information as he read; tuning in to punctuation cues to support how the sentence should be read to give it meaning; and looking for evidence in the text to support his predictions and conclusions. Sam still had difficulty with inferring beyond the literal level of fiction text, but he made considerable gains in his comprehending of nonfiction books and articles. We attributed this to his love of nonfiction, which was a strong motivating factor. Our work with Sam is still going on.

Reflection

We can't let children like Sam slip between the cracks just because they are quiet and well-behaved and give the appearance of successful reading. When a teacher encounters a child who reads by calling the words with little comprehension, she must teach in ways that foster the student's acquisition of comprehension strategies. The teaching of reading doesn't end when children hit chapter books; they're still learning to read in the upper-elementary grades (Sibberson and Syzmusiak 2003). And many students need very explicit teaching as they build their repertoire of strategies for solving words and understanding text. We have to help fill their toolbox with ways to stay engaged and interact with text.

Our goal for a child such as Sam is for him to head off to middle school with an attitude that says, "I am a reader who checks on his own understanding; a reader who makes attempts to solve problems when meaning is lost. I have ways I can employ to fix my confusions and to make sure I understand what I read." The rest of this chapter describes in more detail the lessons that were used in Sarah VanderZanden's fifth-grade class to help Sam and many other readers who were struggling with comprehension issues.

Only the Reader Can Monitor His Own Comprehension

For years teachers have thought it was their job to check on the students' comprehension of material with questions. We've asked students to write answers to the questions at the end of the chapter; we've written our own questions, ones we think are even better than the ones in the book; or we've run modified discussion groups, but when the students don't talk, we end up asking a series of questions. Teachers often tell me, "I have to ask questions. How else will I know if the students have done the reading or not?" Ellin Keene, coauthor of *Mosaic of Thought* (Keene and Zimmerman 1997), says it's time we stop "checking on comprehension" and instead start devoting our energies to actually teaching ways to enhance students' comprehension.

In reality, questions often don't give you the information you are seeking. A reader is capable of answering questions without ever having understood what she read. A colleague of mine at the Center for Equity and Excellence in Education, Elizabeth Powers, created this example. Try reading the following passage and then answer the questions at the end.

Tiz and Tot at the Blague

Tiz and Tot are frips. They like to scrumble together. They like to scrumble at the blague. Tiz is building a blaguehop. Tot is scrumbling in the glup. Tot plorkes Tiz with glup. The glup is cold. Tiz skadoodles!

"Stop that!" Tiz says. "I do not like it when you plork cold glup on me."

"I'm sorry," Tot says, "but it's funny to hear you skadoodle."

Comprehension Questions
1. What are Tiz and Tot?
2. Where does this story take place?
3. What do Tiz and Tot like to do?
4. What did Tot do to Tiz?
5. Why did Tot do this?
6. Would Tiz and Tot be good frips for you?

You can answer all of these questions and yet not have understood what you read. You can't draw a blague, nor do you know what glup is. And you don't know if Tiz and Tot are children, old people, caterpillars, or even aliens! Though you answered the questions with 100 percent accuracy, you have no meaning behind what you read.

If the teacher is not going to be the one to check on the child's comprehension, then who will? The reader, of course. Prior to teaching children ways to aid their comprehension, the control of checking on under-

standing must be placed in the hands, and minds, of the students themselves. Cris Tovani warns us, "When we assume the sole responsibility for
monitoring comprehension, our students gladly relinquish control over
their reading" (2000, p. 35). Now we see how Sarah's mini-lesson on this
topic plays out with her fifth-grade class.

<table><tr><td>MINI-LESSON</td><td></td></tr></table>

Whose Job Is It to Monitor for Understanding?

For the purpose of getting a discussion going with her students about self-
monitoring for comprehension, Sarah used an idea from Cris Tovani's
book *I Read It, but I Don't Get It*. Tovani suggests, "Share real-life examples
of professions that require practitioners to be aware of their thinking"
(2000, p. 47). Here is how Sarah implemented that idea.

Sarah opened the lesson by writing the word *comprehension* on a whiteboard. She asked the students to discuss what it means. The students'
answers, as she expected, all related to reading. In order to expand on the
students' definition of comprehension, Sarah continued the lesson like
this:

Sarah: You are all correct that comprehension means understanding what
you read, but comprehension doesn't only apply to reading. It is part
of everything we do in life too. Let's take a doctor, for example.
Suppose there is a doctor who goes to a meeting where he is supposed
to learn about a new medicine—what it's for, who should take it, what
disease it will help, and so on. But the doctor doesn't really understand what the presenter is saying and he leaves the meeting without
understanding the facts about this new drug. So, tell me, what do you
think might happen when the doctor goes back to his office and
begins prescribing this new medicine?

Quinn: He could give it to someone who's not old enough to have it.

Oscar: Yeah, he might kill somebody with it.

Maria: Why didn't he ask somebody to explain it better?

Sarah: That's what I was wondering, Maria. If you don't understand something you should stop and do something about it because if you don't,
matters could only get worse.

Rylie: That doctor might mess up some people. He should have paid
attention.

Sarah: I agree. Let's think about another profession. What about a baseball player? Have you ever noticed how the coach always does those

hand signals? (*Sarah mimics a baseball coach touching his cap and pulling on his right ear.*) Each of those movements is supposed to signal the baseball player to do something, like steal second base or throw a curve ball. What if the baseball player didn't understand the signals?

Robbie: He could lose the game for the team and, boy, would they be mad.

Sarah: Exactly. If you don't understand something, boys and girls, you have to stop yourself and do something about your confusion. Think about the two examples I just gave you. Turn to your partner and talk about another possible example. Think of an incident where a person who doesn't comprehend should stop himself, and if he doesn't, he could only make matters worse. (*The students turn and talk to a partner and then share their answers with the whole group.*)

The students came up with several ideas—reading a recipe and not understanding how to do measurements or what a certain ingredient is; driving a car and not understanding the road signs; being a babysitter and not understanding the instructions of how to change a diaper; and cleaning houses and not understanding that the wood floor doesn't get washed with soapy water. After each one, Sarah confirmed that if the person did nothing to clear up her confusion, matters would go from bad to worse. After sharing ideas, Sarah made the analogy to reading. "It's exactly the same thing with reading, boys and girls. If you don't understand what you are reading, you need to *stop* yourself and do something about it. If you don't, things will only get worse." Sarah concluded the mini-lesson in this way:

Sarah: That's how it's going to be in our classroom, readers. During reading workshop time, or anytime that you are reading, I want you to keep a constant check on your understanding. I can't get inside your head and tell you to stop because you are confused. Only *your* brain can do that. You have to be the checker! Keep asking yourself, "Am I getting this? Does this make sense to me?" If you don't comprehend what you're reading, then you must stop and do something about it. That will be your first job as a reader in this classroom. There will be no pretending you understand when you don't, OK? My job will be to show you lots of ways to help yourself fix up your reading when you are confused. In fact, I'm sure many of you have some great ideas for that already. Be thinking about what you do to help yourself comprehend as you read today. Tomorrow we're going to talk about some of the techniques you are already using.

In this conclusion, Sarah is sending the message that it's OK to get confused in this classroom; it happens to all readers at some time or other. The important thing is that you have to be aware of when you are confused and make an attempt to do something about it. Sarah is also preparing the students for the next day's mini-lesson topic, when they will share some of the fix-up strategies they already use.

What If You Don't Know What a Word Means?

There are many times when students pronounce a word in the text, but have no concept of its meaning (for English language learners this can occur quite frequently). A word such as *cantankerous* is fairly easy to sound out—can-tank-er-ous—but probably not familiar to most students. The meaning of a whole passage is not always lost because of one word, but many times it is. Stopping to look up words in the dictionary may not be an effective use of time. And oftentimes the dictionary definition is more confusing than the word itself. I remember laughing hysterically when Frank McCourt described his dictionary fiasco in *Angela's Ashes.* As a young boy he decided to look up the word *virgin* in the dictionary. The definition contained two words he didn't understand, and then the next definition contained two or three more. It turned into a wild-goose chase, and he finally gave up! Since dictionary definitions don't always explain meanings in ways that children can understand, students can benefit from learning how to get a sense of the word from the context in which it was used.

MINI-LESSON Using Context Clues to Figure Out Word Meanings

I began this lesson with two objects that are difficult to identify without seeing how they are used in context. I showed the objects to the students, then told them two stories about these items. I held up the first one (a red kitchen aid called a "silicone grabber," which covers only your fingers and thumb and is used like a pot holder). I played around with it in front of the children, thinking aloud about what this could possibly be, bending it, making all kinds of suggestions, but never saying what it really was. Then I said, "One day I was at my neighbor's house having a cup of tea. All of a sudden the buzzer on the oven went off. My neighbor jumped up, grabbed this, put it on her hand, and pulled a hot tray of cookies out of the oven. Like that, instantly [I snap my fingers], I knew what this object was!"

I then held up the second object (a bright green paper holder weighted with sand). Again I wondered out loud about what this object could possibly be as I shook it and noticed the slit in it. "Then," I said to the students, "when I saw my sister blow-drying her hair and reading an article at the same time, I immediately grasped its meaning." As I said this, I stuck a journal article in the paper holder. The children could see how you would be able to read without using your hands to hold the text. "My sister told me she had another one of these in her kitchen to hold her recipe cards while she's cooking."

Next I asked the children to turn and talk to a partner about what helped me *know* these objects. (A few students misunderstood and talked about what they thought the objects were. I helped them by explaining the task again.) When we came back together, two students shared their answers with the whole class.

Callan: You had to see it being used to figure it out.

Sean: You guessed a lot of different things it could be, but until you saw someone use it, you weren't sure.

Pat: You're right. I had to see it being used. (*I wrote the words* In Context *on the overhead projector.*) It was the context that surrounded the object that helped me know what it was. Context gives things meaning; context is the situation or the circumstances surrounding a thing. This same idea, students, works with understanding difficult vocabulary words that you might come across as you're reading. Let me show you what I mean. (*I put a list of words on the overhead projector that I was fairly sure none of the fifth graders in the room knew*—odious, crowed, slavered, brogans, cronies, *and* cleaved.)

Pat: What if I said we are having a test on these words right now and you all need to write down the definitions of these words?

Students: (*in chorus*) What? No way! Can we copy from the dictionary? I don't know any of them!

Pat: Don't worry. We're not really having a test. I know that these are hard words, and what makes them even harder is that they have no context. There is nothing surrounding each of the words to give them some meaning. But I'm going to take these words and put them in context for you. All these words happen to be in a story that I'm going to read aloud today. The story will give these words some context. With the information from the sentences surrounding each of these words, you won't have any trouble figuring out what they mean.

I then led the children over to the storytelling corner and read *Caleb and Kate* (1977) by William Steig. It's a wonderful story about a man and wife who argue a lot, but still love each other. One day a witch turns the husband into a dog, unbeknownst to the wife. Kate takes in the stray dog, not realizing it is her husband, Caleb. It takes a year before he finally becomes himself again.

During the reading of the story, I didn't stop to talk about the difficult vocabulary words. That came later. I kept meaning at the forefront by asking students to periodically predict what they thought would happen. I wanted them focused entirely on the story line to build the context.

After the story, we returned to the overhead area to continue the lesson. I put the following text (a passage from the book containing the word *odious*) on the overhead projector.

> During one of those crazy quarrels, Caleb got so angry he slammed out of the house hating his wife from top to bottom; and she, for her part, screamed after him the most odious insults that came to her mouth.

I used this excerpt to model. I first covered over the difficult vocabulary word, then read aloud before it and after it. I underlined some of the other words in the sentence that were giving me hints (*quarrels, screamed, insults*). I continued thinking aloud about what could replace this word. I put in the words *mean, nasty,* and *hateful* in place of *odious* and tried the sentence out. I asked the children if they thought that made enough sense to continue reading. They agreed it did.

Next, I asked the students to turn and talk with a partner about what it was I did to help myself get to the meaning of the word. With guided discussion, we created a chart (see Figure 5–1).

When you come to a difficult vocabulary word:

1. Cover it up.
2. Read what came before the word and after the word.
3. Think about another word or phrase that would make sense there.
4. Reread it all with that new word or phrase in place of the difficult vocabulary word.
5. Decide if that makes sense. (If it does, you probably have a good idea of the meaning of the word.)

Figure 5–1
Context Clues
Chart Created by
Daisy Bokus and
Her Third Graders

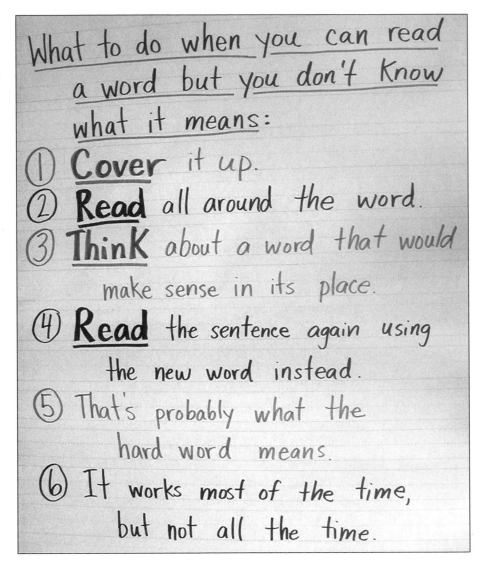

What to do when you can read a word but you don't Know what it means:

① **Cover** it up.
② **Read** all around the word.
③ **Think** about a word that would make sense in its place.
④ **Read** the sentence again using the new word instead.
⑤ That's probably what the hard word means.
⑥ It works most of the time, but not all the time.

The next overhead was a page from the story that contains several difficult words—*crowed, slavered, brogans.*

And there at her feet, instead of a snoring carpenter, was a snoozing dog. "What a darling spell!" she crowed; and pleased to have worked her day's worth of mischief, the witch departed, swollen with pride.

It was sundown when Caleb woke. First he yawned, then he stretched, then he reached to scratch in his armpit. With his leg? Holy gazoly! His eyes bulged and his big mouth hung open and slavered. Where he should have seen a belt and breeches and a pair of heavy brogans, he beheld the belly and hairy legs of a dog!

In order to begin turning responsibility over to the students, we figured out these three difficult vocabulary words together as a shared demonstration. I did the reading and then students followed the chart, made suggestions, and built on each other's ideas. I offered support when necessary.

The final overhead was of the page containing the word *cronies*. To release responsibility even further, I asked each child to come up with an answer on his own.

Whenever their friends came calling, Kate would show off her dog. He enjoyed these gatherings, the human conversation, but he didn't like to have his head patted by his old cronies.

No one had any trouble with this one.

Finally, I sent the children off to work with partners on a sheet that contained the text of three different scenes from the story. I put eight words in italics (*sill, thrust, strove, bereft, deftly, pried, mongrel,* and *fend*). The children began their work and the room filled with talk. They used the technique described on the anchor chart to help them. I was not as concerned about the students completing the entire sheet as I was about the kinds of conversations they were having. Listening to their talk acted as an assessment time for me and the classroom teacher as we circulated around the room with clipboards in hand for anecdotal note taking. We needed to know who understood the concept of context clues and who didn't. The next day, we planned to come back together to share our thinking about the meanings of the words on this sheet.

Notice the pattern of teaching in this lesson. I didn't just tell children what to do by saying, "Context clues are important, boys and girls, so if you are stuck, read all around it and you might get the word meaning." That's not enough for most children. Instead, I began by building a sense of what "context" was, connecting it to real-life experiences. Then I made the analogy to reading difficult vocabulary words. I had fun with the students, pretending we'd have a test, but then illustrated my confidence in them by saying, "You will be able to figure out these words after the story is finished." I walked them through several examples, gradually passing the responsibility for doing the reading work over to them. For some children, this one anchor lesson and having the chart hanging in the room for reference will suffice. Struggling readers will most likely need more practice using context clues with support from the teacher. We planned to build on this lesson in guided reading sessions and when working one-on-one with students.

When I share this lesson in workshops with teachers, two questions often come up.

1. Do you follow up this activity by having the children use a dictionary to see if they inferred the meanings correctly?

No, I don't. The purpose of this lesson is not to learn the meanings of these specific words, but rather to learn a process that can help them while reading. It's the thought process, the strategic activity of inferring meanings of words from context, that I want students to take on, not the ability to use these particular words correctly on their own. Although I think using a dictionary is an important skill, I don't want it to get in the way of learning about using context clues. Readers use context clues "on the run" while reading continuous text, usually when there is no possibility of researching the exact meaning with a dictionary.

2. This seems like a long mini-lesson. Are all your anchor lessons this long?

No, usually lessons are much shorter. Most of my strategy lessons take about five to fifteen minutes and are done right before reading workshop begins. However, an anchor lesson this long is sometimes unavoidable. If you did this lesson all the way through as I have written it, it could take thirty minutes or more because it includes the reading of a lengthy picture book and a follow-up partner activity. It's time well spent if you get a lot of mileage out of the lesson. For example, just think of how often throughout the year you would be referring to that chart or using the ideas from this anchor lesson in guided reading lessons or individual conferences with students. However, the lesson can also easily be divided over several days as the chart shows.

Day One	Day Two	Day Three	Day Four
Read aloud the text for enjoyment.	Introduce with the objects; model one example; make chart together.	Follow the chart and do three examples together with the students.	Have the students work with partners on the practice sheet.

William Steig is a great author to use for doing a context-clues-modeled lesson. He consistently uses high-level vocabulary words in his stories.

Many of his other books also work as well as *Caleb and Kate* when doing this lesson. For instance, *The Amazing Bone, Sylvester and the Magic Pebble, Dr. DeSoto,* and *Brave Irene.*

Guiding a Group of Struggling Readers Through a Novel

Did you ever notice that the readers who struggle spend a lot of their time hopping from book to book, never quite finishing one or even getting very far in many of them? They often choose nonfiction texts because they don't have to read the book from beginning to end. Rather, they can open to any section and find a few facts that interest them.

I worry about these students never experiencing the joy of a whole text, like the books the other children in the class are reading. By not experiencing "a good read" from beginning to end, they never get the opportunity of realizing what sustained comprehension feels like. Some readers need guidance and support through a longer text. I believe that hooking them into a really great book is a powerful motivator for becoming a lifelong reader. For these reasons, I like to do a novel unit with a group of struggling readers in upper grades.

Most teachers of reading are aware of the work of Lev Vygotsky. He says that the best teaching and learning take place within the child's zone of proximal development (ZPD). The ZPD is that place where the child can perform the task with the help of a more capable Other; in other words, the teacher acts as a cognitive coach. Carol Lyons, in her book *Teaching Struggling Readers* (2003), builds on this concept by saying that teachers need to *create* more opportunities for working with children within their zone of proximal development. To me, supporting a group of struggling readers through a novel is a perfect way to create such a ZPD opportunity—a place where the students can learn to comprehend better with the support of a more capable Other (Vygotsky 1978; Lyons 2003).

Usually I use short text for guided reading opportunities, but once in a while doing a chapter book accomplishes things that a short text can't. A chapter book allows students to make predictions, but they then have to change their predictions as new information is acquired. It allows them to see characters develop and change over time; to identify plots and sub-plots; and to look for conflict and tension, problems, and solutions in the book. By periodically discussing the book with others, students help each other comprehend. It's purposeful reading over a sustained length of time. I treat the novel unit as a series of guided reading sessions.

By simulating guided reading sessions you can keep the format predictable:

- Introduce the chapter or chapters the same way as you might do a book introduction for emergent or progressing readers on a shorter text. Tell the students a little bit about the next chapter; then ask a question to hook them in or stimulate discussion.

- Have a teaching focus for each chapter or chapters. The focus is a way to support the group members in becoming better readers. Regie Routman (2003) says we should always be thinking, "How is what I am doing today going to help students become more independent readers?" The focus might be rereading, reading on and coming back, using context clues, visualizing, paraphrasing, or any other strategy or behavior that proficient readers use. Be sure to tell the focus to your students. For example, "Remember we've been working on making pictures in our mind as we read. Practice doing that today—make a movie in your head about what the characters are up to in this chapter."

- Set a purpose for the reading of each section. A purpose is more text specific than the overall focus. For example, "Read to find out why the characters seem so mad in this chapter" or "As you read, think about the relationship between this character and his dad; is it similar or different from a relationship you have with a parent?" Sometimes give the students a specific way to respond, such as a T-chart or a sketch, which they are then to bring back to the group to stimulate conversation.

- Have the children do the reading on their own; each child has a copy of the text. The teacher might work one-on-one with specific students, offering guided support on parts of the reading.

- Bring the group back together for discussion after each assigned section, usually a day or two later. The students negotiate the meaning of the text by sharing opinions, supporting conclusions and predictions with evidence from the text, making connections, and asking questions to clarify meaning and clear up confusions. As part of this talk, the teacher also guides the students in discussing the focus of the lesson.

By following the above suggestions teachers can support many upper-grade students who are struggling. The most important point here is to match the students appropriately to texts as best you can. All chapter books are not the same. They differ in length, vocabulary, sentence structure, inferential level, and in other challenges they may present to students. We need to choose carefully and offer support when needed.

Techniques Versus Strategies

The word *strategy* has been applied to many different concepts in literacy over recent years. Its overuse has resulted in confusion; for example, there was debate over the difference between a skill and a strategy. My concern is the confusion that results when teachers use the same word *strategy* for (1) the in-the-head thinking that proficient readers do naturally as they read and (2) teaching ideas, such as KWL, Venn diagrams, and reciprocal teaching. Because I am ultimately concerned that teachers understand the *network of strategies* a reader needs to construct in order to learn to read, it is important to be clear about this term and not use it to describe a whole host of things.

I reserve the word *strategies* for the thinking a reader does to help himself read and understand a text. Readers *predict* words, they *self-monitor* their reading, they *link* parts of unknown words to other words they know, they *visualize* information in text, they *infer,* and so on. Teaching ideas, on the other hand, are *not* strategies. They are the techniques or tools teachers use to get certain kinds of thinking going in the head of the learner. I'm not trying to stir up a semantics argument here. Rather, I think the distinction helps teachers understand more about the reading process and about how to assess students' construction of the reading process.

Graphic organizers, data retrieval charts, KWL, and other techniques encourage the kind of thinking proficient readers use automatically. For example, the first part of a KWL chart—"what do we *know* so far?"—is meant to activate children's schema or prior knowledge of a topic, to bring out children's thinking. It's the thinking that matters, not the tool. For struggling readers, the thinking (the in-the-head strategic activities), not the tools, causes some of their problems. Children who struggle with comprehension are not doing the kinds of thinking that proficient readers do as they read.

With this in mind, I introduce and use many teaching techniques to struggling readers as scaffolds to nudge them to do the thinking necessary for comprehension. Many literacy experts refer to these as ways to help students hold on to their thinking (Harvey and Goudvis 2000; Tovani 2000; Miller 2002; Wilhelm 2001). The following teaching tools are just a few of the ways to encourage students to do the thinking that results in comprehension.

♦ Highlighting text—this idea from Cris Tovani (2000) can be used as a way to nudge children to pay attention to their own self-monitoring abilities. Give students an article or short passage of text (one they can write on), and ask them to highlight everything they *do* understand with one color highlighter pen and everything they *do not* understand with another color. The process of physically marking the text forces the children to think about their reading, making decisions related to their comprehension. Children can bring their marked text to their discussion group. This serves as a springboard for discussion about the text.

● "Say something" is an idea from Short, Harste, and Burke (1995). When students are partner reading, one child takes a turn being the reader. After a designated section or certain number of paragraphs, the other child turns to his partner and says something about what's been read. Then the children reverse roles. The tool encourages students to talk about the text while they are reading and together negotiate its meaning.

● Coding text is suggested by Beth Davey (1983) and many literacy experts as a way for children to hold on to their thinking and bring that thinking back to the discussion group. Rather than overwhelming readers who struggle with too many codes, I start by using only four.

1. ✓ I understand this.
2. * I have a thought. (This might be a connection, a prediction, a feeling, a question.)
3. + I think this is very important information.
4. ? I'm confused here.

● The patterned sentence—I think _____ because _____—is suggested in *Becoming One Community* (2004) by Fay and Whaley. Ask students to make entries in their response logs after reading and bring them back to guided reading or novel unit groups. The pattern encourages students to make predictions and inferences or draw conclusions (in the "I think" section) and then provide evidence from the text or from their prior knowledge (in the "because" section).

When asked to use these techniques, students must stop at points in their reading, have a thought or response, and manually record it or code it. In a way, it slows down the reading process; it lets struggling readers in on the secrets of what proficient readers are actually doing as they comprehend. These readers don't have to do the manual process forever. Eventually the marking of text gives way to a voice in the head interacting with the text; the voice in the head, or self-talk, eventually gives way to mere thought—that is, comprehension (Vygotsky 1978; Lyons 2003; Tharp and Gallimore 1988).

We return to these techniques and others often when working with struggling readers. We use them in other subject areas, such as science and social studies, and in various classroom contexts, such as guided reading, whole-class mini-lessons, and shared demonstrations with lifted text on the overhead. The techniques are extremely valuable ways to support struggling readers, but are not the end goal.

As stated earlier, I've elaborated on the distinction between teaching techniques and strategies because it helps teachers understand what we are assessing students for. What is the end goal that we want struggling readers to reach? We want students to take on the strategies independently, not just use the tools or techniques. Students may demonstrate prior-knowledge thinking or make connections when reading with you, but may not do so on their own. Assessing a student on an assigned highlighting or coding activity is only a stepping-stone. What we are really looking for is evidence that a child has taken on the thinking, the strategic in-the-head activity, that will help him comprehend text better when reading independently.

I encourage teachers to stay with a focus long enough to observe the transfer to students. We need to take that extra step. In *Strategies That Work,* we are reminded that "using the language isn't enough" (Harvey and Goudvis 2000, p. 189). Children can say, "I made a text-to-text connection" or "I made picture in my mind" and still not be able to comprehend. Harvey and Goudvis give examples of teachers working with students to articulate how and why a given strategy enhanced their understanding. We can't just teach about making connections, visualizing, and asking questions as we read. We need to help children over the hump to the point of thinking, "How did *making that picture in my mind* help me understand the setting better?" "How did *making that connection* get me to understand this character better?" "How did *asking those questions* keep my mind on the information presented in the text and help me decide what was important?" When our students can answer these questions on their own, then we have gone the final mile.

In Brief

- Individualized conferences can help teachers discover which students might be having problems self-monitoring for comprehension.

- Help students understand their job of stopping when meaning breaks down.
- Teach children ways to distinguish between easy, just right, and challenging texts so that they make appropriate choices of books on their own.
- Explicit teaching of context clues will help children figure out difficult vocabulary while they read.
- Techniques such as highlighting or coding texts are tools teachers can use to support student strategy use.
- Novel units, done as a series of guided reading lessons, are one way to support struggling readers with sustained comprehension over time.
- All children need to feel they are part of the "literacy club."
- Teachers can teach *for* comprehension strategies rather than just asking questions to check on understanding.
- When we teach a strategy to a struggling reader we need to stay with it long enough to see that the child has taken over the strategy and uses it independent of the teacher's prompting.

CHAPTER 6

Self-Monitoring
in All Ways, *Always*

To help understand the multiple self-monitoring processes that occur as we read, I make the analogy to the way all of us constantly self-monitor for so many things as part of daily life. Drivers keep a watchful eye on their speed, the cars in front and behind, the traffic signals, the signs, where they are in relation to where they are headed, and even the sounds and feel of the car to make sure that nothing is going wrong. A golfer like Tiger Woods keeps a constant check on his grip, stance, swing, shoulder movement, and follow-through. And what about a chef like Emeril? Have you seen him noticing the consistency of the sauce at the same time as he measures ingredients, monitors the temperature of the oven, and checks the freshness of the foods involved? He's a whirlwind of motion around that kitchen, monitoring and regulating all aspects of the cooking experience. Multiple monitoring is something the human brain is quite capable of.

Readers also self-monitor for many things as they engage with text. The following are just a few examples:

◆ Am I making sense?
◆ Did what I just read look right?

- Did it sound right?
- Am I reading the punctuation correctly?
- Are the questions I have about this text getting answered?
- Who's talking now?
- Where are these characters?
- Who or what do the pronouns refer to?
- Did what I predict happen or do I need to rearrange my thinking?
- Which information is important enough for me to remember?

When listed like that, it's a wonder any of us learned to read, and yet it's an automatic process. More often than not we self-monitor simultaneously on multiple levels. While we don't actually voice the questions listed here as we read, we are subconsciously aware of them and would stop if some dissonance occurred.

For children who struggle, it's not all that easy, and doesn't come quite so naturally. For them it may seem a monumental task to monitor for all these reading variables. That's why they need teacher support as they learn to integrate all the self-monitoring processes. Sometimes they need explicit teaching in order to get a particular type of self-monitoring under way. For example, in Chapter 4 we saw how Justin learned to self-monitor for when he was sounding choppy so that he could repair his lack of fluency. And in Chapter 5 we followed Sam and other students as they learned to take more control over self-monitoring for their understanding.

In this chapter we look at some other ways in which a reader must self-monitor. First, I take Beatrice through the framework as she breaks her habit of inefficient sounding out and learns to better self-monitor for visual information. Then I offer some ways teachers can teach self-monitoring behaviors to beginning readers or readers struggling at emergent levels. Finally I share lessons to help children whose lack of self-monitoring causes them to lose track of characters, dialogue, or setting.

Self-Monitoring Through the Lens of One Child

Here's What

Beatrice is a delightful, very chatty third grader who loves to read, but benchmarked slightly below grade level at the beginning of the school year. She's a hard worker and employs many strategies when reading, but still struggles to keep up with classmates. Daisy Bokus, her teacher, has been documenting Beatrice's steady progress. When I began working with Daisy using my framework for struggling readers, her focused look at Beatrice brought to the forefront a habit that this student exhibited— Beatrice would attempt to sound out unknown words by guessing random sounds and creating nonsense words. The sounds she made (beyond the beginning sound) were often not even represented in the word. Some typical running record errors looked like this:

Child:	strurvis	flings	dreesed	bowl	blakes
Text:	stumps	ferns	dashed	pile	packs

Under normal circumstances, one would expect that reading nonsense and continuing on would seriously affect a child's comprehension. What was especially interesting about Beatrice was how much she was able to comprehend despite this habit. While reading fiction Beatrice loved to stop and chat, talking about the story and making connections. She would make comments about what the characters were doing or predictions that, for the most part, fit the story line. But as we focused our attention on Beatrice's comprehension more intensely, sifting through what she was actually saying, Daisy and I agreed that she tended to be fairly general in her comments and retellings. She got the gist of the story, but missed some finer details because of the misread words.

So What

During the reflective stage, Daisy and I agreed that Beatrice was doing a fairly good job of using context clues; she definitely read for meaning most of the time. On many occasions, even with a nonsense word, she was able to maintain the sense of the story. From a comprehension standpoint, this was a plus. But because we often listened to her read aloud in one-on-one conferences, we noticed the habit of making random sounds when she came to unknown words. Our conclusion was that Beatrice was ineffective in her use of visual information when taking words apart. Though she had the basics of letter/sound correspondence, she was not able to use that information when the words were multisyllabic or new to her. We decided that the focus of our teaching would be to:

♦ get Beatrice to become more aware of her habit and encourage her to stop making random sounds when encountering unknown words;

- make sure she read past the word and came back to it before engaging in sounding out to prevent loss of meaning;
- teach Beatrice ways to look at visual information of words more effectively.

Now What

In order to get Beatrice to become more aware of her habit and break it, Daisy and I would stop her and say back to her what she had just read. Since she was not doing the monitoring, we had to start by doing it for her.

Beatrice: (*reading about crickets*) "On a hot day, crickets make so much noise so quickly that it's hard to count the number of chisss ters [chirps]."

Daisy: Beatrice, let me tell you about something you've been doing a lot lately. When you come to a word you don't know, you start making sounds, any sounds, and make up a word. Listen to what you just said. (*Daisy repeats the sentence as Beatrice read it.*)

Beatrice: (*laughing*) What are chisters? (*She is quite aware that it is not a real word.*)

Daisy: That's what I was wondering! If it's not something that makes sense, you can't just throw in any sounds. What have we been working on when we come to words we don't know? (*The teacher points to the class context clues chart, which Beatrice has actually done very well with during the shared demonstration lessons.*)

Beatrice: Pass it, put in something else, and make it make sense.

Daisy: That's right. Readers need to use the information in the sentence to think about what the tricky word could mean.

Beatrice: I do that when I'm reading by myself, when I read in my head.

Daisy: You do? That's great. You can do it when you are reading aloud also. What do you think this word means?

Beatrice: (*reads the sentence before and after*) It's the noise that the crickets make.

Daisy: Yes, that's right. Crickets make a sound called a chirp. I want you to try that—pass it and put in a word or phrase that makes sense—*before* you start sounding out so you don't lose the meaning of what's happening. Then come back and take a closer look at the word. I can help you learn how to take these words apart so that you get closer to the correct pronunciation. OK? That's what we'll work on for the next few weeks. But you have to stop doing that crazy sounding out. Agreed?

Beatrice is such an easy student to work with. Daisy and I often comment on how she takes exactly what we've explained to her and works on it. Over the next several days she became much more aware of the random sounding out she was doing and tried hard to stop herself. If she started doing it, we would sometimes hear her catch herself and read past it first. One day when Daisy was taking a running record on a section of text, Beatrice started making some random sounds, stopped herself, and then looked up at the teacher and said, "I was hoping you didn't hear that!" We knew she was on her way to self-monitoring that habit out of existence!

While we were raising Beatrice's awareness of her habit of creating nonsense words and encouraging her to use context clues more consistently, we began to help her learn to look at print more effectively. We felt that she was looking at some, but not all, of the letters in the words that stumped her. She was not showing any evidence of noticing familiar chunks in words. She was also confusing some letters, such as, *b, d,* and *p.* Following are several types of supportive interventions and prompts that we began using with Beatrice.

1. We always kept a small whiteboard, marker, and eraser on hand. When Beatrice got stuck on a word we would quickly write it larger on that board, breaking it apart for her, while she read past it to get a sense of the meaning. We would say, "Take a look here, Beatrice, and see if this helps you with that tricky word."

| fi   nal   ly | | fl   o   ck |
| in   vis   i   ble | | ch   ir   p |

    Notice that not all the words have been broken into syllables. With one-syllable words, we separated the beginning blend or digraph from the middle chunk, and then added the end letters. Sometimes seeing the word written larger and separated like that was all she needed to solve it.

2. At other times we would need to write an analogy for part of the word, that is, a word Beatrice knew that contained the same part. The known word was written above the similar chunk in the unknown word.

| day | | eat |
| spr   ay   ed | | b   ea   m |

We'd say, "You know this word. Can you use part of it to help you with the middle of that tricky word?" Beatrice had always been successful at making analogies with simple words, such as, *man* to *fan* or *not* to *lot*. She needed more experiences with trying that same linking process with parts of longer words.

3. Another technique that helped was to have Beatrice break apart and examine words she already knew. After reading a text we would pull out several words that she had read correctly—*carpenter, escaped, nervous,* and *vacation.* She clapped the word parts first, listening for which part she would write as she divided the word. Conversations around these words strengthened her knowledge of how words work. We talked about how each syllable always contained a vowel; how certain pairs of letters were almost never broken apart, such as *th* or *ch*; or how common endings like *tion* and *ous* stayed together. Using known words helped her concentrate on the *process* of breaking words into parts. When students are learning a new process, it's easier for them to do it with familiar information.

4. Eventually we began transferring the responsibility for making the analogy to Beatrice. For example, when she stopped on the word *rustled* in a sentence, I asked, "Can you find a part that's like another word you know?" Beatrice used her thumb to show *rus* and said, "It's like *bus.*" Even though I had to help her with the rest of that word, she was showing us that she was starting to look at a larger chunk rather than just at the first letter. In addition she was attending more carefully to print rather than making random sounds.

5. We occasionally used the prompt "Show me a part you are sure of" to encourage Beatrice to make careful decisions about which part of the word she was seeing clearly. This helped her narrow and focus her attention on the other parts of the word that were giving her the most trouble.

6. We held Beatrice accountable for checking on similar-looking letters before making a sound for that letter. We said, "Beatrice, you know you sometimes mix up *b/d/p,* but you know how to check to determine which one it is. You need to decide which one it is first *before* making the sound." The classroom teacher had taught Beatrice ways to confirm confusing letters the previous year. Beatrice had an index card on her desk with Bb, Dd, and Pp on it, which she used for this purpose. Whenever children become lax in doing part of the reading work that they are already capable of doing, we need to remind them that it's part of their job.

7. Another way to direct her attention to the part of the word she was mixing up was to underline the parts she pronounced correctly. When she said *appuncterate* for *appreciate* we wrote it like this on the whiteboard:

ap	pre	ci	ate

We'd say, "You got the first and the last part right, but let's look more carefully at the middle."

Keep in mind that not all words in English can be decoded phonetically. For that reason we encouraged lots of flexibility with this process. Children need to know, especially with vowel sounds, that they may have to make a few tries. Since Beatrice was just learning how to take words apart we often offered her the correct link. For example, if the word she was stuck on was *height* we would give her the analogy of *night* (what it sounds like) as opposed to *eight* (what it looks like).

The process of taking a word apart is meant to get the child close enough to the sound of the word, allowing meaning to help the child determine the word. For example, a child who knows the word *prowler* in his oral language but does not recognize it in print can try sounding it two ways—with the *ow* sound, like *cow* and with the *ow* sound, like *snow*. Once he's done that he could choose the correct pronunciation of the word based on the meaning of the sentence. However, if a child doesn't know the meaning of the word *prowler* because he is a second language learner or an English speaker who never heard that word, then he would not be able to use meaning to confirm which pronunciation is correct. He could only get confirmation from the teacher or another student.

Many of the words that Beatrice had trouble with were words she did not use in her oral vocabulary. We always took time to talk about the meanings of these new words and concepts, such as leaves *rustling*, the *beam* of a flashlight, the *stump* of a tree, or *prowlers* in the house. It's important to attend to meaning even when the focus of your instruction is searching for further visual information. Balancing all three sources of information—meaning, structure, and visual cues—is always the goal.

Then What

Keeping the focus of our instruction the same over several weeks served Beatrice well. She learned more about how to solve words that she had never seen before. Our running records showed that little by little the habit of random sounds and nonsense words faded away. We saw many more substitutions that made sense. We also documented the many times she read past the word and came back before attempting sounding out. Her decoding efforts showed evidence of using chunks of the word rather than just individual letters.

On the rare occasion when the random sounding behavior did surface again, we noticed it was always when the text was too difficult for her. This solidified in our minds how important it is to keep children in a range of texts that allows them to use their system of strategies effectively. We were also alerted to think back to our own book introduction to see if there was some way we could have supported the child better.

Reflection

When I reflect on this experience with Beatrice, I am reminded of when I learned how to sign. Trudy, my friend and neighbor who is deaf, began teaching me sign language twenty years ago. In the early years, Trudy was careful to sign slowly to me so that I could understand everything she was saying. But occasionally I would watch conversations between her and her husband. Their hands and fingers would fly! I would get the gist of what they said, but in order to improve as a signer, I had to learn the vocabulary and expressions I was missing. It's the same with Beatrice. Passing over some words and just getting the gist of the story wasn't enough. To improve as a reader, she needed to learn the specifics of taking apart the new vocabulary she was missing.

What I would consider the most beneficial result of the Beatrice story came from the thoughtful reflection of the classroom teacher. Daisy told me that when she first realized Beatrice's ineffective habit, her impulse was to focus exclusively on meaning. After our discussions she realized that she would also need to teach Beatrice how to use visual information better *while maintaining meaning*. In addition, Daisy shared that this intense focus on taking words apart with one struggling reader made her think about her overall literacy program. Although she was confident in the way her reading and writing workshops were developing, she now knew she needed to add more word study to her curriculum. We discussed places in her day where this could happen, such as right after morning message, after a shared reading or during a shared writing experience, or before writing workshop. Some professional books that serve as excellent resources for these types of mini-lessons are:

Word Matters: Teaching Phonics and Spelling in the Reading/Writing Classroom
(1999) by Gay Su Pinnell and Irene Fountas.
Word Savvy: Integrated Vocabulary, Spelling, and Word Study, Grades 3–6
(2004) by Max Brand.
Spelling K–8: Planning and Teaching (1999) by Diane Snowball and Faye
Bolton.

Next we backtrack to another type of self-monitoring that needs to be
in place with very early emergent readers. We don't wait until children are
in third and fourth grades reading chapter books to teach self-monitoring.
Self-monitoring is a strategy that needs to get under way at an early age.
The next section addresses the questions, "What should beginning readers
or struggling readers at emergent levels be self-monitoring for?" and "How
do you teach self-monitoring to these students?"

Widening the Lens: Self-Monitoring with Emergent Readers

As young children begin to construct a system of strategies for figuring out
words and understanding text, most of them naturally begin to self-monitor for the following:

- One-to-one matching of voice and print
- The pictures and the words, to make sure they match
- Whether the story is making sense
- The beginning letter/letters of words
- Their known words

Struggling readers at the emergent level don't always self-monitor well for
some of these things. However, with explicit instruction and by creating
opportunities for practice, teachers can support these children as they
take on self-monitoring behaviors at a very early stage.

Self-Monitoring for Voice/Print Match

One of the first things teachers model with beginning readers is direction-
ality, moving left to right across the page, along with the one-to-one matching of words and speech. It's a common occurrence in kindergarten and
first-grade classrooms to see teachers demonstrate this by pointing underneath words during shared reading with Big Books, morning messages, or

poems. Sometimes individual children hold on to the pointer with the teacher to get the feel of pointing to each word, matching print and voice. Children are encouraged to notice spaces between words when we are reading together and to use spaces as they write each day in writer's workshop.

For some children who are only beginning to make sense of the printed code, the early experiences of reading with the teacher and touching under each word help them notice "black blob, white space, black blob, white space," and so on. Children who are fluent speakers may not necessarily realize where words separate in oral speech. You've probably heard funny stories of children who blend words together into one word, such as, "and to the republic for Richard Stands" and "the dawnserlee light" as Ramona does in Beverly Cleary's books. Young children don't always know where one word ends and another begins.

To support understanding the concept of a word, which contributes to awareness of voice/print matching, teachers can perform a variety of activities:

- Have a child come up to the morning message to circle his name in the text. Say, "Show us where your name starts; shows us where it ends."
- Do a variety of activities with names. Say, "Jonathan's name is a *word*. Let's count the letters in this word. Is his name a long word or a short word? Let's clap the parts of his name."
- Use highlighter tape to bring children's attention to high-frequency words in Big Books or poems. Say, "Who can find the beginning of this word? Who can find the end? Who can show us a space between two words?"
- Have one child put up his hand to *be the space* before another student writes the next letter or word in an interactive writing session.
- Make a book with exaggerated spaces between words. Tess Pardini, a first-grade teacher and coauthor with Emelie Parker of *"The Words Came Down!"* made one, which is reproduced in part in Figure 6–1, and in Appendix B in its entirety.

The majority of children pick up on the concept of one-to-one matching quite easily, but for some readers more effort on our part is necessary. When a child's control of voice/print matching is still shaky, it's quite common to see the student elaborate on the number of words in the text. Take a look at this example. The child has acquired the pattern of the text from

Figure 6–1
Exaggerated Spacing
Helps with
Voice/Print
Matching

Look   at   the   tiger.

the teacher's book introduction. She reads using the pictures to determine what changes in the sentence on each page. But look what happens on page four.

Child: Page 1 I am eating.
         Page 2 I am drinking.
         Page 3 I am sleeping.
         Page 4 I am talking on the telephone.
Text's actual words: I am talking.

This is a perfect opportunity for the teacher to bring the child's attention to the print to help her notice how many black blobs were actually on that page!

Mike was a struggling reader in first grade who continued to think reading was merely a matter of memorizing early pattern books. He looked very little at visual information. One day I introduced a book about favorite foods and we read it together. The next day he grabbed the book out of my hands, saying, "I know this one" and started to recite what he thought were the words of the text by just looking at the pictures.

Mike's reading: I like pizza.
                 I like hot dogs.
Text's actual words: I like to eat pizza.
                      I like to eat hot dogs.

I quickly stopped him before he went any further.

Pat: Mike, hold on a minute. Something's not quite right here. Let me show you something. On this page you said, "I like pizza." (*As I said these words I counted them on my fingers.*) But look how many words are on this page. Count them. (*He counts out five words.*) Hmmmm. Something's not right, don't you think?

Mike: (*looks at me, unsure what to do. He seems to be thinking, "This is strange. I thought I had this book all memorized."*)

Pat: (*taking out a dry-erase board*) Let's try something. I know you are an expert at writing the word *to*. (*Mike can write only four words at this point*—Mike, mom, I, to.) Write *to* for me here. (*He does it.*) Now check it. Are you right?

Mike: *To.* (*runs his finger under the word and says it as I've taught him to do when he writes words on the whiteboard.*)

Pat: Great. Now find the word *to* on this page. (*He does it.*) And find it over on this page. (*He does it several times.*) I *knew* you were an expert on *to*. Now, start to read this book again, using your finger, but when you get to that word *to*, be sure your mouth is saying *to*.

Mike: "I like" (*a little hesitation*) "to eat pizza." (*As he reads, Mike gets a bit of a surprised look on his face when he reads the word* to, *as if seeing it for the first time. He continues reading the words of the text correctly, touching underneath each word.*)

Pat: (*when he finishes reading the whole book*) What a great job you did! You were checking with your finger to make sure the words you were saying matched the words of the book.

In this example, I was helping Mike learn to self-monitor for one-to-one matching in several ways. I made him aware that the number of words on the page was different from the number he said. I modeled the dissonance that should have been part of his thinking but wasn't when I said, "Hmmmm. Something's not right." Then I focused on a word that I knew he could read and write. I was encouraging him to use his known words to help him read text correctly. Next I asked him to use his finger to read because this brought his eyes to the print rather than just looking at the pictures. This attention to noticing when things are not matching, self-monitoring for one-to-one and for known words, must begin very early. For struggling readers who neglect to do this type of monitoring, we need to teach explicitly and create opportunities for them to practice early self-monitoring behaviors.

There are two ways to support children as they begin to self-monitor for visual information at emergent levels. One is to make simple books with them. The second is to move children out of early patterned texts (see Figure 2–4: Fountas and Pinnell levels A and B, Reading Recovery levels 1 and 2) and into more challenging texts, which are not as easy to memorize and have more opportunities for self-monitoring practice (Fountas and Pinnell levels C and D, Reading Recovery levels 3 through 5.)

Making Books to Encourage Self-Monitoring Many school districts provide their teachers with an adequate supply of books to use with readers at emergent levels. Others, for whatever reason, do not. Making books for or with children alleviates some of the problem of not having access to books appropriate for beginning readers, older readers who are functioning at emergent levels, or some English language learners. We can make books in a way that encourages the reader to monitor for early visual information, such as voice/print match, known words, first letter of the word, their own name, or names of siblings or friends.

I simply cut three pieces of unlined (8½-by-11-inch) paper in half, add a construction-paper cover, staple it together, and I have a six-page book. This is an easy job for parent volunteers. One year I had six volunteers who liked to help by working at home, some of whom were non–English speakers. Each volunteer made one hundred blank books. We divided them up among all the primary teachers, so that every K–2 teacher had a pile of blank books. A teacher could just reach for one when the need arose.

When the child is just beginning to learn to look at print, I start by making a book using the "I/name" switch.

I like hamburgers.
I like Coke.
Sandy likes apples.
I like bananas.
Sandy likes ice cream.

Each line of text appears on a different page. A picture, drawing, or sticker is added to each page as a meaning cue. Don't waste time on drawing. Find ways to move that part of the book-making along quickly by using stick figures or easy drawings. You and the student can create the text for these books interactively, with the child writing any sounds she is capable of, and you writing the rest. Or you can make a book ahead of time to use when reading with the child.

Notice how the switch of "I" for the child's name is random. When the child reads this text, she must monitor for when it says, "I" and when it says, "Sandy." Even that little bit of self-monitoring pushes the child to do some reading work. Children know when they are beginning to really make sense of the print on their own. A reader like Mike feels a sense of pride when he knows he is actually reading the words and making sense of text, and not just reciting the book from memory.

Later I vary the pattern of the text so that it's necessary for the child to pay even more attention to the print. In order to vary the pattern you can:

- Put the child's name in a variety of places. They usually know their name quite well and will be able to search for it in different places. For example, "'I like pizza,' said Anthony"; "Giovanni, do you like to skate?"

- Use high-frequency words with both upper- and lowercase letters. For example, try starting the patterned sentence with a high-frequency word, such as, "Is this a _____?" "In go the _____." "My mom can _____." Students need to see that My/my and In/in are the same words.

- Make the last page of the book slightly harder, breaking the pattern, even if it means you have to support the child on that page by reading it together. This allows you to give more meaning to the text. The story is actually about something, rather than just a pattern. Many times we try to make it funny on the last page or sometimes we just write a question. Some examples of last pages are: Come on! Let's go! Look out! Run! Oh, no! What a mess! What fun! Which animal do you like best?

- Add number words to the text. Example text:

  I can see one sun.
  Nataly can see one moon.
  I can see five stars.
  Nataly can see eight stars.
  Mrs. Johnson can see four stars.
  Look at all the stars!

  The change in the subject, the number, and the break in pattern on the last page require the child to carefully monitor.

- Add the word *and* on random pages. Sample text:

  I like hamburgers.
  I like pizza.

Gavin likes tacos.
I like milk and Coke.
I like hot chocolate.
Gavin likes Pepsi and Sprite.

Because there will be multiple pictures on those pages the child will automatically read the word *and* even if it is not yet a known word.

♦ Use children's names from the class, the teacher's name, or names of family members. We find that emergent readers can handle having various names of people they know in the texts. Many can even write the names of their siblings (see Figure 6–2).

Figure 6–2
Student Book,
Wendy Likes to Paint

I like to paint a dog.

Gerson likes to paint trees.

Wendy likes to paint a cat.

Jose likes to paint a house.

Mrs. Johnson likes to paint a car.

We love to paint!

- Make books with hidden windows, a favorite among most children. Use small pieces of sticky notes to hide the answer to a question. The pattern of the book may be "I see a hippo." "Do you see a hippo?" "Yes" or "No" is hidden under the sticky note. If the answer is "Yes," then a picture of a hippo must be there. If the answer is "No," then just the word is there.

- Use common sentence patterns rather than just a phrase on each page. Some patterns that work well for bookmaking are:

I am _____.
I can _____.
I like _____.
I see _____ or I can see a _____.
Look at the _____.
Here is a _____.
Here comes a _____.
Do you like _____?
Is a _____ in here? (Yes or no under the flap.)
This is a _____.
In Ms. Hatchey's class, we like to _____.
We can _____. or We like _____.
Come and see the _____.

Remember to vary the pattern on some of the pages of the book, forcing the child to self-monitor.

Books made by publishers at early-emergent levels tend to hold fast to patterning all the way through the text. These patterns are great for getting one-to-one matching awareness under way and for giving the children a sense that the pictures and the words of text must match, but the rigid patterns don't allow for enough self-monitoring on the part of the child. By making books for or with children, you are able to hold the difficulty to a level the child can handle, and at the same time add some challenges that enable the child to practice self-monitoring.

Providing Support When Moving Students Up in Levels The other way to encourage self-monitoring with struggling readers is to move them quickly out of early-emergent-level texts into later-emergent-level texts. As previously mentioned, books with no breaks in the pattern (typical of early emergent levels) encourage children to memorize rather than look at the print and use some visual information to guide their reading. If we want them to learn to self-monitor right from the start, then we need to give them something they can self-monitor for. This shift to slightly more challenging texts may be a stretch for some students and will require extra support from the teacher.

I used to be hesitant about doing this, worried that there was too much print in later-emergent texts or that the book would have too many sight vocabulary words that the child had never come across. However, experience has shown me that students can benefit when you keep in mind the following points:

1. Give a strong book introduction to set the child up for success with the book. This means giving a brief summary of the text and letting the child talk about the pictures. Also, use some of the phrases from the book in your part of the conversation. (Book introductions are explained fully in Chapter 7.)
2. Practice the awkward language structures or unusual book language ahead of time. Have the child repeat them and get the feel in her mouth of how that structure sounds. Some teachers use the phrase "in the ear and out the mouth." Let the child hear it and say it.
3. Support the child on the first reading of the text, guiding his reading. Use prompts that enable the child to use his strategies and behaviors.
4. Help children with character names. Sometimes a book seems more difficult for a child than it really is because it's just a matter of being able to pronounce the names. It's also fine for the child to substitute a name if that helps him read the book more fluently. A child will usually pick a name that begins with the same letter and is the correct gender.
5. On occasion, do the same book a second time with a fresh book introduction and guided support as a child reads.

Teachers who try this or watch me as I do it with a child from their classroom are frequently surprised at how well the child did. The real proof comes the following day, when the child succeeds on a running record with 90 percent or above. Teachers realize how much more the child has been exposed to in this slightly higher text and how much more opportunity the child has had to practice self-monitoring as well as other strategies for solving words and making meaning. The book then goes into the student's book box, and he can reread it during familiar reading time. Oftentimes, the child is so excited about reading a nonpatterned text with a story line that he is highly motivated to read it again and again.

Self-monitoring is one of the strategies that we teach right from the start. By using some of these suggestions even the earliest emergent readers will come to know that it is part of their job to do the checking and confirming—for one-to-one matching, for known words, for making words and pictures match, for initial sounds, and for making sense of the text. This early work sets the tone for continued self-monitoring. As readers move up in difficulty of texts, they become more astute at monitoring for other aspects.

Self-Monitoring in the Upper-Elementary Grades

In the framework example of this chapter we watched Beatrice learn to self-monitor for further visual information beyond the first letter while maintaining meaning. This is just one piece of the whole picture in the network of strategies. Self-monitoring problems that struggling readers in the upper-elementary grades often face are another issue. It's easy to notice a student who is not comprehending, but a bit harder to dig deep and discover what caused his confusion.

- Did the student lose track of the characters, setting, or action of the story?
- Does he know how to visualize or ask questions of the text in order to stay engaged?
- Is he having trouble following the dialogue?
- Is he unable to infer and use his background knowledge along with hints from the author?

Self-Monitoring of Characters

One way that some older struggling readers become confused as they read chapter books is by losing track of the characters. This can happen to anyone, even a proficient reader. Once I was reading an article in *Newsweek* magazine (January 14, 2002) about an American woman married to a bin Laden operative. The author sometimes used the first name of the husband and wife, Wadih and April, but at other times referred to them by their last names, El Hage and Ray. I was reading along just fine until all of a sudden I read, "says Brown." I thought, "Who is Brown?" I had to turn back a few pages and find the reference that explained that Marion Brown was April Ray's mother. I somehow had missed the reference or was concentrating so hard on the main characters that the minor ones got lost. I share stories like this with students to show them that the things that confuse them can also confuse proficient readers.

Many adult readers appreciate the family trees that are placed in the front of novels that contain an enormous cast of characters. I was especially thankful for such a list last summer when my book group decided to read *Anna Karenina* by Leo Tolstoy. The Russian names were difficult enough to pronounce let alone remember. The chart helped me keep Alexei Alexandrovich Karenin and Alexei Kirillovich Vronsky straight.

I never realized how easily this idea of character lists and family trees could be transferred to children until I read *Still Learning to Read: Teaching Students in Grades 3–6,* by Franki Sibberson and Karen Szymusiak. The authors discuss how they created a classroom chart with students when reading aloud *Holes* by Louis Sachar. This novel has characters from three different subplots, so the class made an anchor chart to keep them straight.

I immediately tried this idea with a group of fifth graders who were listening to their teacher read aloud *Flying Solo* by Ralph Fletcher. This book, about a class of sixth graders who decide to run the school day on their own when their substitute doesn't show up, has many members of the class as characters. Together we came up with a phrase or two that encapsulated each character's personality or the special information that made that character unique (see Figure 6–3).

After making the chart for *Flying Solo,* a few of the students decided to make a character list for the individual books they were reading. Two struggling readers, Minh and Jose, were reading *Year of the Panda* by Miriam Schlein, and said they were having trouble with some of the Chinese names in the text. They made their own index card of character clues, complete with a pronunciation key, and used it as a bookmark (see Figure 6–4).

Keeping Track of Characters During Dialogue

It's also not uncommon for some children to lose track of characters in passages containing lots of dialogue. Here is a sample lesson I modeled in a fourth-grade class. I demonstrated what I use to help myself stay focused in lengthy or confusing dialogue parts.

Figure 6–3
Chart of *Flying Solo* Characters

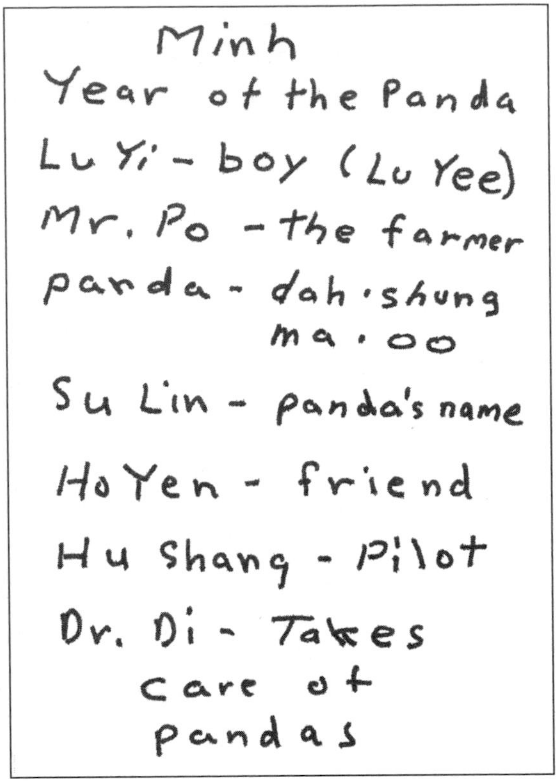

Figure 6–4
Minh's Bookmark Card of Characters

MINI-LESSON   Who's Talking Now?

I began this lesson by sharing two excerpts from a book I was reading, *Drowning Ruth* by Christina Schwarz. The students always seem to love it when I bring in an adult book that I'm reading to begin a lesson for them. I first reviewed how we know *when* someone is talking (quotation marks) and how we know *who* is talking (a speaker tag, such as "Jim said," usually tells us.)

As I put the first page on the overhead projector I elaborated on what I was noticing about the dialogue in this text.

"What happened to that baby?" Ruth said suddenly. She held her fork in the air, a beet slice skewered on the tines.

No one responded for a moment, as Amanda and Carl decided whether they were relieved or annoyed to be distracted from their argument.

"What baby?" Rudy asked finally.

"More tomatoes, Rudy?" Amanda held out the plate.

"The baby we took to its mother," Ruth said. "How did it get lost?"

"A lost baby?" Carl said. "Who loses a baby?"

"She must be talking about a lamb," Amanda said.

"I'm not talking about a lamb. It was a baby and it was crying, so we brought it to its mother."

"The stork brings the baby to the mother," Rudy said.

"No," Ruth said, "we did, Aunt Amanda and me."

"Aunt Amanda and I," Amanda corrected.

"Maybe you read it," Carl said, "in a book."

"That girl, always the book," Rudy said.

Pat: In this first example, I notice that after every time there is some dialogue the author tells me immediately who is doing the talking with a speaker tag. (*I highlight where I see quotation marks and begin underlining all the character names in the speaker tags.*) Ruth said this, Rudy said this, Amanda said this, Ruth said this, Carl said this. (*I continue down the entire page.*) Naming the character like that makes it easy for me to follow who says what, doesn't it? (*I put a second page up on the overhead.*) But look what the author did on this page. These three quotes have no speaker tags at all. (*I point them out with my marker on the overhead and write "no tag" next to each.*) The next one says, "she said," and then one more says, "he said." That's a bit confusing, wouldn't you say? There is not one character name mentioned in a speaker tag. So what should I do?

"Tell me who Imogene's father is."

"Why, George Lindgren. You know that."

"No. And Mary Louise is not her mother. I know about the baby, Amanda. Tell me who the father is."

"How . . . ?" she began.

"Who is he?" He said it gently but firmly, as if speaking to a child.

After taking some of the students' suggestions, I explain how I gather information presented previously in the text to determine which characters are present in this part of the story and then I envision the scene.

Pat: It's a little bit like when I watch an episode of *Friends*. On TV I can see all six of the friends sitting around the coffee shop. I know who's talking because I can see them on the TV screen. With books, I have to envision scenes just like that in my head. Here I can picture Carl and Amanda in the house. I know that they are the only two present during this scene, so the "he" must be Carl and the "she" must be Amanda. I make a mental picture of this scene as it's happening, like a TV show in my mind. (*I continue the lesson by also teaching the students about the writing convention of indenting each time a new character speaks. I demonstrate how, knowing this, I can follow who is talking when there is no speaker tag available.*)

Next I use a part of a text that I worked on with a group of students in a guided reading lesson earlier that week. The students did an excellent job that day figuring out which character was speaking, so I let them explain their thinking to the rest of the class.

Toward the end of the lesson I turn the responsibility for doing the reading work over to the students. I put up the last example on the overhead projector. This one comes from *Babe: The Gallant Pig,* by Dick King-Smith. (Teachers who try this lesson should use a page from the book they are reading aloud to their students at the time.) I give each student a copy and let them work with partners to figure out who's talking in this excerpt. We come back together to share ideas of how they figured out which character is speaking which sentence.

"It's nice, dear," she said to Babe. "I've still got you."

But not for all that long, she thought. Poor little chap, in six months or so he'll be fit to kill. At least he doesn't know it. She looked at him fondly, this foster child that now called her "Mum." He had picked it up, naturally enough, from the puppies, and it pleased her to hear it, now more than ever.

"Mum," said Babe.

"Yes, dear?"

"They've gone off to work sheep, haven't they?"

"Yes, dear."

"Because they're sheepdogs. Like you. You're useful to the boss, aren't you, because you're a sheepdog?"

"Yes, dear."

"Well, Mum?"

"Yes, dear?"

"Why can't I learn to be a sheep-pig?" (1983, p. 29)

At the conclusion of this particular lesson, one student suggested that another way to help keep track of who is talking is to change your voice to match the characters. We experimented with a quick Readers Theater activity. One child read the Mother Sheepdog parts, another was Babe, and a third student read the narrator parts. After that demonstration we talked about how a reader can make character voices in his head as he reads silently.

Learning about visualizing scenes and how authors give hints to indicate which character is talking are ways of helping children self-monitor for character information. I'm thankful that authors who write for children are still using quotation marks. The last three adult books that I read did not use any quotation marks, even though the books were filled with dialogue (*Eventide* by Kent Haruf; *Teacher Man* by Frank McCourt; and *A Million Little Pieces* by James Frey). I'm still baffled by this current trend and am not really sure if it is the author's decision or the publisher's. However, I dread the day when this new trend makes its way down to children's books, giving us yet another way to confuse our struggling readers!

Self-Monitoring Related to Setting

My own personal preferences as a reader lead me more toward realistic fiction, memoirs, and historical fiction than to the science fiction or fantasy novels that my husband enjoys. I have a difficult time picturing the setting of out-of-this-world places with their unusual creatures. I'm one who prefers seeing *The Lord of the Rings* movies over reading those texts. Of course, on the rare occasion when I do read in that genre, I have taught myself to pay attention to the descriptions, visualize carefully, and look for hints that the author is offering about where the characters are in time and place. For struggling readers, however, time and place can become confusing because they haven't learned how to follow an author's hints concerning setting changes.

MINI-LESSON | Following Setting Changes

I began a lesson in Kara Conques' third-grade class by talking with the students about what setting means and how we know where the characters are (see Figures 6–5 and 6–6. These are my writings on the overhead as I talked with the students).

Figure 6–5
Setting

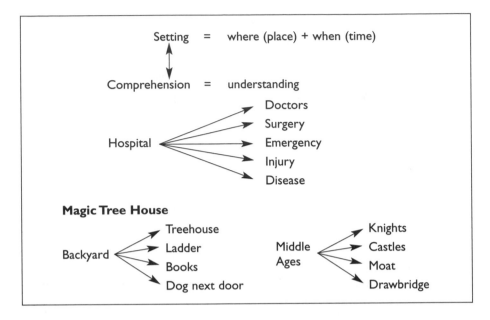

Figure 6–6
Authors Give Hints

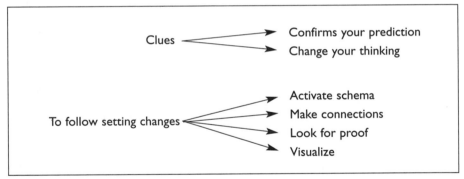

The children knew that setting relates not only to the place, but also the time period of the book. We discussed that being aware of the setting can help you predict words that might appear in the text. For example, if the setting of a story was a hospital, the students predicted that the author might use words such as *surgery, doctors, emergency, injury,* and *disease.* I had them quickly turn and talk to a partner about the setting of the book they are presently reading. A few students shared the setting of their book and how they knew.

The main part of the lesson was a shared demonstration. I used an excerpt from *The Great Cheese Conspiracy* (1989) by Jean Van Leeuwen. My goal was to guide the students in looking for evidence in the text that helps a reader determine where the character is. Following the movement of the character aids in understanding what's happening in the story.

The children had already learned from Chapter 1 that the characters, a group of mice, live in a movie theater. The mice, guided by their leader, Marvelous Marvin, were planning to become big-time thieves by pulling off a dangerous heist. In the first three pages of Chapter 2, the setting changes three times. I put an excerpt on the overhead:

The Great Cheese Conspiracy
by Jean Van Leeuwen
2
I Go Outside

Faster than a speeding bullet, I head down the aisle toward the side exit, staying under cover to escape detection. I slip easily between feet and umbrellas and packages, and once in a while an empty shoe. Another time I might have stopped to rearrange all this, but today I am all business. A true professional.

A moment later I am lurking under a seat across from the little red sign that reads "Exit," waiting for someone to go out. But no one is budging at the moment. The cartoon has them glued to their seats. I pace the floor, eager to get on with my adventure.

Watch what happens as I encourage children to search for hints in the text to serve as proof of where the character is.

Pat: Look at the title and tell me where you think the character Marvin will be in this chapter. (*I cover the words of the text beyond the chapter title.*) What's your prediction of the setting of Chapter 2?

Andy: He's going to be outside the movie theater because it says, "I Go Outside."

Carolina: Remember the other rat said it's dangerous out there because no mouse has ever returned from there.

Pat: So our prediction is that the mouse will be outside and there might be danger. I'm going to start reading this page and you can follow along. Try to notice when you hear something that confirms our prediction or if you hear something that tells us we were wrong in our prediction and you'd like to change your thinking.

I purposely picked this excerpt because I knew the students would predict one thing and then have to rearrange their prediction as the evidence unfolded. A few hands start to go up as I read the phrases "down the aisle" and "toward the exit sign." More hands go up when I get to "lurking under a seat."

The children then turn and talk to a partner to discuss their ideas. The majority of them realize that Marvin the mouse is not outside; he's still in the movie theater. But a few children have become confused. I heard Stefani tell her partner, "I heard *packages* so I know he's out on the street near stores 'cause that's where you get packages." Isn't it interesting how some children get their mind stuck on one prediction and then try to make everything fit that idea?

As we share our thoughts, we guide those students who were not able to see the evidence that Marvin is still in the movie theater. I underline phrases the students notice that support their thinking. Some children find ways to prove their point that I hadn't even thought of.

Hamza: It said no one is budging because they're watching the cartoon. And the cartoon is on the movie screen.
Georgia Mae: Yeah and he paced the *floor,* not the ground. If he were outside he'd be on the ground.
Neil: I was thinking that since it said he was eager to get on with his adventure, that's a hint. If he was already *on* his adventure, he'd be outside, but he's just waiting for his adventure to start, so he must still be inside.

Next I read most of the second page and ask the students to think about where Marvin is now.

My eye falls on a shopping bag resting temptingly on its side beneath the next seat. I can't resist such an easy target and slip inside for a quick snack.

I sink my teeth eagerly into something soft, something rather dry, something that sticks to the roof of my mouth. I spit it out. It's a ball of knitting yarn. I've stumbled into a knitting bag.

I know right away I'm wasting my time. I start to take my leave when a strange thing happens. The bag tips, throwing me to the bottom where I land sharply on a couple of knitting needles. As I start to pick myself up, the bag begins to move.

I notice during the turn and talk that more children are helping each other come to the correct conclusion with evidence from the text. They mention key words and phrases that back up their decision. Almost all conclude that Marvin is in a shopping bag filled with knitting materials. Raphael, however, thought that since it said "quick snack" the mouse must be in the refreshment area of the movie theater. I reread the whole paragraph containing the words *quick snack* and the other children help him clear up his confusion.

Pat: Let's come back together, boys and girls. Here's what we've figured out so far. In the beginning of Chapter 2 we discovered that Marvin was on the floor of the movie theater, and then he was in a shopping bag of a lady who was leaving the theater. Now, I've given each of you a copy of the next part. I'll read and you can follow along on your copy. As I read, feel free to underline on your copy any hint the author gives you to indicate where the mouse is now. Remember, by giving our attention to the setting we can visualize and comprehend what is happening in this story.

I let the children work independently as I read the passage, then give them a few minutes to work with a partner, and finally we share out ideas as a whole group. The students are excited about how much proof they found and all want to talk.

At the end of all my lessons, I try to give the students time to process what they learned. Sometimes this means making an anchor chart together, but on this day we debriefed by turning and discussing answers to the following questions with a partner:

- What did we learn and talk about today?
- How will this help you as a reader?
- What can you do to practice this as you read in your own books today during reading workshop time?

The students need time to process what they have learned and determine how it will help them as readers. It's not enough to take one strategy, such as self-monitoring for setting changes, and just teach it to the students. We need to help them integrate it into a working system of strategies for comprehending.

Diego: If you know the setting, you know where the characters are.
Raphael (an ELL student): When you read you have to *imaginary* [his word] what's happening in the story.
Isabella: If you practice stopping and talking with your friends, it can help you understand the story more.

Anjali: Finding hidden words helps you know the setting. When I read my books I get confused where the people are. This will help me figure out where the people are.

I hope teachers notice how many strategies overlapped in this lesson. When thinking about setting we are using children's schema, making connections, visualizing, and inferring—all at the same time. Though the focus was on self-monitoring for setting changes, the children naturally brought all their other strategies to bear on that task. They activated prior knowledge. Some students made connections to times they went to the movie theater and discussed where the refreshment stand was. They all were able to visualize Marvin inside the knitting bag as the lady jostled up the aisle. This interconnectedness within the network of strategies is what normally happens for fluent readers. Even though a teacher chooses one focus for a lesson, the overlap of the other strategies soon becomes apparent.

In Brief

- All readers monitor for many things as they read.
- Struggling readers often have trouble self-monitoring, but teachers can take a close look at them to discover what the particular issue is.
- Keeping a whiteboard handy to break words apart, providing analogies, and talking about how words work can help readers who struggle with using visual information effectively.
- Self-monitoring needs to be taught even with the very earliest readers.
- Making books for emergent readers creates opportunities for practicing self-monitoring.
- Holding children too long in early emergent texts sometimes encourages memorizing rather than using strategies.
- Teachers can use techniques or helpful ways to support children who lose track of characters as they read.
- Lessons can be developed to focus on any one particular kind of self-monitoring, such as learning to read dialogue better or keeping track of setting changes or movement of characters.

CHAPTER 7

Specific Support *for* English Language Learners

If you have English language learners (ELLs) in your classroom, you already know that there is no one description of a child that fits all. Kathleen Fay and Suzanne Whaley write, "Seeing each child as an individual is at the heart of what we do. We would never assume that all students with learning disabilities or all gifted students are the same, and we should do likewise with English language learners. They are as diverse a group of children as any" (2004, pp. 9–10).

The variety of ELLs is endless when you take all the factors into consideration—literacy level in the first language, years in school in the United States or in other countries, attendance record, parents' literacy, mobility, language or languages spoken in the home, and other opportunities for learning, here or elsewhere. I always try to get as much background information as possible about the ELLs I teach. Such knowledge not only informs my instruction, but also helps me find a way to connect with each child and develop rapport.

Just because a child is learning English does not mean that he will struggle with the process of learning to read. The term *English language learner* is not interchangeable with *struggling reader* (O'Leary 1997). There are many ELLs who are literate in their own language and acquire reading and writing skills in English quite easily. There are others who are unable to read and write in their native language, yet still have no significant difficulty becoming literate in English. Acquisition of literacy for both these groups takes time, good instruction, access to interesting books in a variety of levels and genres, and opportunities provided for practice. But they will succeed.

About 10 to 20 percent of all children seriously struggle with learning to read (Clay 2001). Since classroom populations are becoming increasingly diverse, it makes sense to assume that some of those struggling students would be ELLs. These students are not only learning a new language but also struggling with constructing a network of strategies to figure out words and understand text. The techniques I have described in the first six chapters are applicable to all struggling readers, native English speakers or not. Finding out what the child does at the point of difficulty and using responsive teaching to model, support, prompt, and reinforce the child as he takes on strategies and behaviors are effective ways to work with all children, including ELLs who are struggling with the reading process. Good teaching is good teaching for all students.

I'm often asked, "But is there more that teachers need to know in order to be at their best when teaching English language learners to read?" I respond to that question in this chapter by sharing techniques and ideas that teachers can use to support any English language learner, whether he is a struggling reader or not. Most of my knowledge comes from my reading on the topic as well as the hands-on experience I have gained in the last thirteen years working in two schools in northern Virginia: Garfield Elementary School, where approximately 60 percent of the 380 students are language minority students, and Bailey's Elementary, where 78 percent of the 900 students speak a language other than English as their first language.

The first half of this chapter presents information on the little things you can do to make a difference for the English language learner you are sitting beside and teaching to read. The second half of the chapter addresses the broader issues related to ELLs, includes stories to demonstrate certain points, and suggests other texts where you can find out more.

Teachers New to Working with ELLs

Last year I had the privilege of working with Katie Keier, an excellent teacher new to the school. During Katie's thirteen years of prior experience teaching primary grades, her classes often contained students with special needs—learning disabilities, emotional problems, poverty issues—but she had never worked in a classroom where the majority of students were ELLs. As she began teaching second grade at our school, one of her goals was to learn as much as she could about supporting them as readers and writers. Katie was open to watching me work with some of her second language learners and equally open to letting me watch her. She was also excited about hypothesizing and experimenting with a variety of ways to support ELLs. The sections that follow include some of the things we learned during our year of studying together: first, information on book introductions, because those played a significant role in our teaching; then, common issues in texts that often cause difficulties for ELLs; and finally, a suggested teaching move and sample scenario that Katie and I decided to try.

Book Introductions

In her book *By Different Paths to Common Outcomes,* Marie Clay writes,

> Book introductions are an authentic social interaction about the new book; but when they provide an orientation to novel features of stories and of texts, they are also a kind of teaching.
>
> Readers should remember that although the interaction flows like a conversation and leaves room for the child's input to inform the teacher, it also includes deliberate teaching moves. (1998, p. 175)

Clay defines book introductions first as "social interactions." The teacher begins by giving the title and brief summary. Starting off this way helps activate students' prior knowledge, which facilitates future comprehension. Think of how your comprehension and the ease with which you read something are affected based on whether you have prior knowledge of the topic. After the title and summary, a conversation ensues as the children begin to discuss the cover and the pictures. The children might make connections to something the teacher said in her summary, or they might answer a question that the teacher posed to stimulate interest or inspire discussion. All of this is done conversationally.

Second, Clay says that book introductions are a "kind of teaching" because teachers make "deliberate teaching moves." The teacher can intentionally decide to include some of the vocabulary or language structures from the text in her conversation. The teacher is also listening to what each child is saying to gather information that will inform her teaching decisions. What information or vocabulary does the child have related to the topic? Did the child have a similar experience that will support comprehension of this text? Does the child need clarification or elaboration of terms or ideas before beginning to read?

Several questions arise when discussing book introductions with new teachers. Some wonder why we don't let the children figure out the title. One reason is that the titles of books are often harder than the level of the text. For example, an emergent book's pattern can be: "The bear lives here, the lizard lives here, the alligator lives here," and yet the title of the book may be "Animal Habitats."

Other teachers question the summary part of a book introduction, asking, "Aren't you giving away too much of the story?" The title and brief summary put the meaning of the text in the head of the child so that he can draw upon meaning as one source of information to understand the book and solve the words. Children are "entitled" to a book introduction (Clay 1991). The summary also opens up opportunities for students to connect the ideas in this book to their own prior knowledge. It's been my experience that the summary and conversation stimulate interest in the book and hook the children in and, when asked to read the text on their own, the students do so willingly and enthusiastically.

A book introduction also acts as a way to level the playing field for ELLs. Think about this example. Native English-speaking children who are about to read a text about a boy playing soccer would bring a fair amount of vocabulary with them (*goalie, uniforms, shin guards, goal post, passing, heading the ball*). Many of these terms would not necessarily be part of an ELL's vocabulary. The ELL may know the concepts but not have the English labels for those terms. Therefore, the teacher can use these words in her part of the conversation.

Another question teachers ask is, "The book introductions connected with standardized assessments, like the Developmental Reading Assessment (DRA), are extremely brief compared to the kinds of book introductions you are suggesting. Shouldn't we prepare kids for that testing situation by *not* telling them about the book?" Keep in mind that guided reading is *not* a testing situation. It's instructional time with the student, time to teach and support readers. We don't prepare students for a writing prompt test by giving them constant writing prompts, but rather by developing strong writing workshops that include instruction on writer's process, author's craft, and mechanics. In the same way, we don't use guided reading instructional time to practice for a benchmarking test. We use instructional time to teach reading strategies and behaviors that the child can use on any text, even ones they encounter in a testing situation.

Book introductions were something both Katie and I already used regularly in our guided reading and individual sessions with students. However, our research led us to ask these questions:

- ◆ Is there space in the book introduction for supporting ELLs?
- ◆ What might that support look like?
- ◆ What types of things might be added to a book introduction to support the English language learner's successful reading of the book on his own?

Common Issues

Each of the next six sections describes a common issue that can be found in books for beginning readers, an issue that sometimes causes added problems for ELLs.

Awkward Language Structures

In many books for young readers, we find structures that are very different from the way we speak. Some examples are:

Home we go now.
Off they went to the zoo.
Away went the ball.

Each of these is unlikely to be used in normal speech, but is fairly typical book language. It is difficult enough for a native English speaker to feel comfortable with these phrases; for an ELL the phrases are even more awkward.

Suggested Teaching Move Use the awkward language structure during your book introduction as you are chatting with the student before he begins to read. Tell the student that it's a different way to say it. Then have the child practice saying the awkward phrase as often as needed. Finally, give an example—both *in* and *out* of the text—explain how the phrase will be used in the story, and then give another example of how it might be used in the child's life.

Example: I gave a brief summary of a book about a family heading for the beach as part of a guided reading lesson with four second-grade children. One of the children was Lucinda, an ELL. I knew that I would need to support Lucinda with an awkward structure that appears in this text. I invited the children to talk about a time they had gone to the beach or anything they knew about the beach. We discussed being afraid of the waves, digging in the sand, and how hot it was. I continued.

Pat: It was hot the day this family went also, so they needed their sun hats. Do you know what sun hats are, Lucinda?

Lucinda: Yeah, so they don't get all the sun on them and it hurts.

Pat: Yes, it does hurt if you get sunburned. Well, can you believe it? They forgot their sun hats, so the dad had to turn the car around and go back for them. When he turned the car, this is what he said: "Home we go now." Can you say that?

Lucinda: Home we go now.

Pat: It's kind of a funny way to say they needed to go back home. Home we go now. Everyone, say it again.

All: Home we go now.

Pat: It's a little bit like if Lucinda and I were walking to school together and she forgot her backpack. I would say, "Home we go now, Lucinda. We have to go back and get your backpack. Home we go now."

Lucinda: (*giggling*) Yeah. Home we go now.

What I was doing here was not merely having the child memorize a line of the text ahead of time. Instead I was giving the child an opportunity to "grapple with the novelty" of such an unusual phrase (Clay 2001). This opportunity not only gave the child a chance to feel that phrase in her mouth, but also helped her acquire the meaning behind the phrase.

I once watched a video of Kathleen Fay doing a similar book introduction with Esmelda, a first-grade ELL reading emergent books. The phrase Kathleen was having Esmelda practice was "Away goes Rabbit." When Esmelda first attempted to repeat the phrase, she said, "Away *comes* Rabbit." So they practiced a few more times. After Kathleen talked with the student about why the rabbit was running away to hide, she then gave an *out of text* example. "When all the kids in your class are running out to the playground for recess I might say, 'Away goes Willie; away goes Tamika; away goes Abdufata.'" Because of the practice time and examples, Esmelda had no trouble reading that phrase when she came to it in the text. My favorite part of the story, though, came later, when Kathleen was shutting down the video camera. She told Esmelda, "You can tell everyone good-bye now because I'm turning off the camera." Esmelda looked into the camera and said with a big smile, "Good-bye, everybody. Away goes Esmelda." She was already adopting that phrase into her oral language.

Irregular Verbs or Advanced Verb Tenses

Many irregular verbs appear in books for young children. It's common to come across sentences such as

The balloon *blew* away.
Nick *swam* across the pool.
The cup was *broken*.

An English language learner who doesn't have these verb forms as part of his oral language might read these as

The balloon blowed away.
Nick swimmed across the pool.
The cup is broke-ded (or broked.)

Along the same lines, many books include sentences with advanced verb tenses such as "it has gone" or "he would have gotten sick." These, too, can cause difficulties for English language learners. We used to think it was unlikely that ELLs would read these irregular verbs or unusual verb tenses correctly until they became part of their oral language. But now many literacy experts agree that children can gain familiarity with some of these language structures through the books they read.

Suggested Teaching Move What Katie and I tried was threefold:

- ♦ Help students notice and practice the new verb structure
- ♦ Provide examples *in* and *out* of the story
- ♦ Give the child a way to solve the unfamiliar word.

As part of our book introduction, we would bring the child's attention to the sentence containing the irregular verb, saying it for him and having him practice it. Then we would talk about how it was used in the book and elaborate on the meaning by using it in another way the child could relate to, similar to what I did in the last instance with "Home we go now." Finally, we would give the child a visual analogy or a mnemonic device, which would aid him in solving the word when rereading the text on his own.

Example: Katie worked with William on the sentence "The balloon blew away." She had him repeat the sentence two times, then continued with an *out of text* situation.

Katie: Suppose you were standing at the bus stop and you had your home-work in your hand. Then a big gust of wind took your homework away. You might say, "My homework blew away." Say that for me.

William: My homework blew away.

Katie: What if you had your hat in your hand and the wind took that away, what would you say?

William: My hat blew away. (*Teacher says it with the child if he needs that support.*)

Katie: Let's find that line about the wind in this book and read it together. (*They do it.*) Now let me show you something about this word so when you're reading this book on your own you'll have a way to figure it out. (*Katie takes out a whiteboard and marker.*)

This last part, giving the child a way to solve the word, is crucial. Without it, the child will likely go back to incorrectly reading the word when on his own. For this instance Katie thought of two options. If *new* is a known word for this child then Katie could use that as a link to the new word. She would write on the whiteboard *new/blew*; they would examine the part that's the same and notice how they rhyme. If she couldn't find a known word with the same part to link it to, she could choose to write *blue/blew* and say, "Even though these two look different at the end, they still sound the same. When you see this word *blew* in the book, think of the color and it will help you read 'the wind blew.'"

Adults use mnemonic devices all the time. For example, when I first met my colleague Stanzi Lowe, she told me how to pronounce her name, saying, "It rhymes with Fonzi from *Happy Days*." I never forgot that. A mnemonic device or visual analogy helps the child pronounce the word correctly when he's reading independently. With this type of support, the chances are higher that the child will practice the verb structure correctly each time he rereads the text.

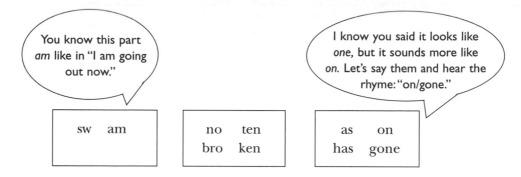

Using the whiteboard in this way is also helpful *while* the child is reading. You can't always anticipate which words or phrases will cause a problem for the child.

With advanced verb forms, some practice time is also needed. Think about what a mouthful it would be for an ELL to read, "Jenna *would have gotten hurt badly* if Josh hadn't dropped the bag of apples." One day I worked with Israel, a second-grade ELL, to support the reading of that phrase. Israel was a strong reader and I knew he would probably be able to read all those words, but I wanted to be sure he had the meaning behind what was happening. During the book introduction, we studied one particular illustration together.

Pat: Can you see what Josh is doing to help little Jenna in this picture?
Israel: He dropped those apples and they went rolling all over.
Pat: Right. And what about the car?
Israel: (*looking at the picture*) That car stopped 'cause he saw the apples Then Jenna didn't get hit by the car.
Pat: So she *would have gotten hit* by the car if Josh hadn't dropped those apples, right? Let's find the sentence about that on this page and read it together.

Vocabulary—Known Words Used in a New Way

Many times ELLs will know a word in one sense, but will not have had experience with that word used in a different context or as a different part of speech. For example,

The mouse was *pleased* that the lion let him go.
The people from the village heard the boy's *cries*.
The blue paint from the sky *ran* into the yellow paint from the sun.

ELLs may know the word *please* to ask for something politely, but may not know it as a verb. They may know about crying tears, but not *cries* used as a noun. Or they may understand that people can run, clocks and computers can run, but not that paint can *run*. An ELL may read the word correctly, but if the teacher senses that the child doesn't have the meaning, a conversation at the moment of confusion can help assist comprehension.

Suggested Teaching Move   In order to help ELLs with words that have multiple meanings, we:

◊   stop the child just after he reads such a word correctly or come back to it later if we feel comprehension was lost. (Sometimes you can only find this out by talking with the child about what's going on in the text.)

◊   teach how to use context clues to figure out what the word could mean in this sentence.

◊   elaborate on the new meaning of the word in this instance.

◊   give another example *out* of the text.

Example: When working with Jasmin one day, I noticed she hesitated on the word *pleased.*

Pat: I see you stopped on that word. Does it look like a word you know?

Jasmin: It looks like *please.*

Pat: You're right, but you have to add the *d.* Can you say the whole word? (*She does*). Now read the whole sentence and we'll think about what that could mean.

Jasmin: "The mouse was pleased that the lion let him go."

Pat: How is the mouse feeling?

Jasmin: He's happy now.

Pat: Why?

Jasmin: Because he thought the lion might eat him, but then the lion said thanks for helping me. You bite the net. So you can go.

Pat: You really understand a lot about the ending of this story. You are probably used to saying, "Please can I have ice cream or please will you help me," right? But that word *pleased* is used differently in this book. Here it means "happy," just like you thought. Let's try reading it with *happy* in there.

Jasmin: "The mouse was happy that the lion let him go."

Pat: Did that make sense? (*She nods.*) Jasmin, what if you cleaned up your whole bedroom—how would your mom feel?

Jasmin: Happy. Really happy.

Pat: We might say, "Jasmin's mom was pleased that she cleaned her room."
(I add a few more examples of teachers and cafeteria workers being pleased with students' behavior.)

Vocabulary—Knowing Concepts Without Knowing the English Labels

On more than one occasion I've heard a teacher say something like this about an English language learner: "He doesn't comprehend because he doesn't know the meaning behind the words. His English vocabulary is so low." When I ask for an exact example, what we realize is that the child *does* have the meaning, but just doesn't have the English label for it. There's a difference. For example, second language learners can often gather the meaning behind unknown words from the pictures or the context of the sentence. When the child is reading, "I can eat my breakfast" in an emergent pattern book, he knows the meaning of the word *breakfast*; he sees the child eating cereal in the picture. He gets stuck on the word because he doesn't know the English label for it. English language learners come to school with years of background knowledge. While their knowledge may be different from a native English speaker's, they still have a wealth of experiences. I try to distinguish between the student who lacks meaning and the student who merely lacks the English word.

At other times, when meaning is not obvious from the picture or context, teachers can still link the new English word to a known concept. For example,

grumbling = talking—The monster went *grumbling* down the road, saying, "I'm never coming back."
peering = looking—"It's not raining," said Bill, *peering* out of the tent.

Though the words *grumbling* and *peering* may not be part of the speaking vocabulary of ELLs, the students are certainly familiar with the concepts of *talking* and *looking*.

Suggested Teaching Move If the word is important to the main idea of the story, we address it as part of our book introduction. For example, if the story was about a rescue we would discuss what a rescue is and use the word often in our conversation. Keep in mind, the word *rescue* can be linked to known concepts for any child. The concept of helping and saving people or animals in danger is common, even if the child is not familiar with that English word or the particular kind of rescue in the story being read.

If the word is not central to the main idea, then we wait until it comes up during the reading or address it after the reading, rather than as part of our book introduction. Our instruction includes the following:

- Using context clues with the child
- Expanding the meaning
- Giving the child a way to figure out the word

First we would support the child in getting a sense of the word from the context of the sentence or general text information. If he was able to fill in a word that makes sense, but didn't quite have the correct meaning or shade of meaning, we would discuss that word further. In that conversation we would hook it to a concept the child knew. Then, we would take a look at the visual information in the word, to give the child a way to help him pronounce it correctly when reading on his own. The following examples will help clarify this point.

Example: Watch how I helped Obdulio with the word *grumbling*.

Obdulio: The monster went *gram bing* down the road. What's that word?

Pat: You're not quite sure of what that word means, are you? Can you put in a word that makes sense? Think about what's going on in the story.

Obdulio: The monster went (*hesitates; checks the picture*) *walking* down the road?

Pat: That does make sense. But while he's walking away remember how mad he is. He's talking to himself, kind of mumbling in an angry sort of way, like he's complaining.

Obdulio: Yeah. He keeps saying, "I'm never coming back. I'm never coming back."

Pat: Let's see if you can figure out how to pronounce this new word that means "mumbling" or "talking to yourself." (*I ask Obdulio if he knows where the word separates. When he shows me with his finger I write* grum bling *on the whiteboard. Above the first part I write the word* gum.) See if this helps you figure out that word.

Obdulio: Grumbling.

Pat: That's right. "The monster went grumbling down the road, talking to himself the whole time." Do you ever grumble, Obdulio? (*He laughs.*)

I know that when I was little and my mom made me eat spinach, I would grumble to myself because I didn't want to.

This student may not fully grasp all the connotations of the word *grumbling,* but at least by our conversation he has grasped the meaning of it in this book and he is starting to understand how it might be used in other instances. That's how vocabulary building works with ELLs. We can't just ask them to look words up in the dictionary and memorize definitions. They need to see and hear the word used in various contexts over time.

Example: Katie supported Josseline with the example of "peering out of the tent."

Josseline: "'It's not raining,' said Bill, peering out of the tent." (*She reads the word accurately during the reading of the text, but marks it with a sticky note, something the teacher has asked her to do with words she's not sure of.*)
Katie: You read that tricky word, *peering,* perfectly, Josseline. Let's talk about what you think it means.
Josseline: Going? He was going out of the tent?
Katie: That would sound right in the sentence, but *to peer* means something different than "going." I could say, "I think I'll peer out the window at the kids on the playground." Or "I'll peer into Ms. Holmberg's classroom and see if they are back from lunch."
Josseline: It's "looking."
Katie: Good job. Now try it in that sentence and see if it works. (*She reads the sentence from the text substituting* looking *for* peering.)

We definitely want ELLs to use context clues when they are reading on their own, filling in a word that would make enough sense so that meaning doesn't break down. Josseline first tried this by suggesting *going* in this instance. If she were reading independently, that substitution would have to suffice. But if we are right there with the child working one-on-one or in a small group, then we should take the opportunity to help expand the student's English vocabulary. Conversations and other examples of the word will help elaborate its meaning. It's not possible to do this with every single unfamiliar word in every story that children read. That's why we always provide pieces of sticky notes for the students to mark words they would like to talk more about when they come back to the guided reading group for discussion time. If they return to the group with no words marked (as often happens when first learning how to use the sticky notes), the teacher can suggest a few.

Vocabulary—Unknown Words and Unknown Concepts

The difference between this issue and the last one is that the ELL not only doesn't know the English label, but also is unaware of the meaning of the concept. Some examples might be: *scarecrow, rodeo, three-legged race, hang-gliding,* or *fencing* (the sport). For some children these not only would be new English labels, but the concepts would also be unknown.

Suggested Teaching Move   Use all the steps from the last example plus an additional one:

- Use context clues with the child.
- Expand on the meaning of the word.
- Give the child a way to figure out the word.
- Use drawings, pictures, acting out, or hand gestures to elaborate on the new concept.

Examples: Here are a few examples of times when we needed to expand the concept of the word with visuals.

1. Because Christian had no idea of what a three-legged race was, I had him stand up next to me and showed him how his left leg and my right would be tied together in this race.
2. Katie brought pictures of people learning how to fence, in their white outfits and equipped with swords, for another group of ELLs.
3. In *The Tiger Rising,* which I read with a fifth-grade group, the character said she was named Sistine because her mom liked the picture on the ceiling of the Sistine Chapel. Because this is referred to many times in that book, I brought in pictures of Michelangelo's painting to show the students.

Figurative Language

The English language is filled with idioms galore—go fly a kite, she screamed her head off, you're pulling my leg, and many more. My suggestion is to discuss them *as they come up* in the texts students read or in other classroom situations. This may differ from what some teachers do. Some may study lists of idioms with their classes all at once. Studying lists of idiomatic expressions is not very effective for English language learners

Figure 7–1
Funny English
Expressions, *Amelia
Bedelia*

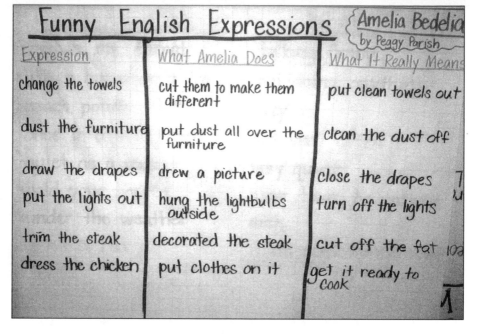

Funny English Expressions {Amelia Bedelia
by Peggy Parish}

Expression	What Amelia Does	What It Really Means
change the towels	cut them to make them different	put clean towels out
dust the furniture	put dust all over the furniture	clean the dust off
draw the drapes	drew a picture	close the drapes
put the lights out	hung the lightbulbs outside	turn off the lights
trim the steak	decorated the steak	cut off the fat
dress the chicken	put clothes on it	get it ready to cook

because it is too overwhelming. Discussing them in the context of what they read allows ELLs to use the context of the whole story to support the meaning of the phrase. Amelia Bedelia books by Peggy Parrish are good examples of texts to use with English language learners both for this purpose and for dealing with known words used in new ways (see Figure 7–1).

Collecting these expressions over time as a class is a good technique. As each new one arises in a text students can discuss it and add it to a chart. I usually let the child who came across the figurative language in a book draw the example and share it with the class before posting it on a chart. The chart sends the message that you can't always take everything in English literally (see Figures 7–2, 7–3, and 7–4).

There are many other facets of English that might cause confusion for ELLs besides the six I've chosen to discuss. The English language isn't an easy one to learn because of its many exceptions to the rules, multiple meanings, awkward sentence structures, and figurative language. My intention in this section is to raise the awareness level of all teachers concerning these aspects of our language. Some things that we take for granted as fluent English speakers need to be examined through the eyes of a young ELL.

Figure 7–2
Collection Chart
of Funny English
Expressions

Figure 7–3
Break a Leg

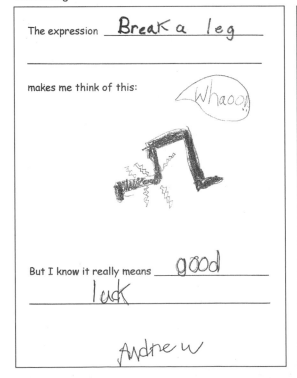

Figure 7–4
Ants in Your Pants

Important Areas of Consideration When Working with ELLs

Consider these four broad topics related to the teaching of English language learners:

1. Becoming a good listener and giving children time to talk
2. Developing classroom communities where ELLs feel valued, accepted, and respected
3. Organizing your classroom to allow time for whole-group, small-group, and individualized instruction
4. Becoming an astute observer of ELLs as they are engaged in reading and writing activities

Listening and Conversing with ELLs

"If the child's language development seems to be lagging it is misplaced sympathy to do his talking for him. Instead, put your ear closer, concentrate more sharply, smile more rewardingly and spend more time in genuine conversation, difficult though it is" (Clay 1991, p. 69).

Marie Clay reminds us to have "genuine conversations" with English language learners. We need to ask real questions about things for which we actually want answers and comment on things that are of interest to the child. Some of us shy away from doing this because we are afraid the child won't understand us or we will have difficulty understanding what he is trying to say. Over the years I have found that it's important to just keep listening, showing interest and concern with your body language and facial expressions, repeating what you think the child is saying, adding words or phrases to support his talk, and then listening some more.

As we converse with English language learners, we need to *elicit, extend,* and *elaborate* (Anderson 1999). Reflecting on those three words has helped me improve my communication skills with ELLs. I know that when I ask questions that have only one-word answers, I'm not giving the student enough opportunity for oral language practice. "Tell me the part you liked about the story" is better than "Did you like that story?" I also know that I need to take time to clear up a child's confusion rather than moving on because we're in a time crunch to finish a given activity before lunch. When I take the time to figure out what's blocking a student's understanding, I become better equipped to make instructional decisions that extend and elaborate his vocabulary or his reading and writing strategies.

Sometimes you can become quite baffled by something a child with limited English has said in conversation, but if you stay with the child and elicit more talk, you can usually figure out what he means. Recently I was talking with a class of second graders about the desert. They were studying the vegetation and animals that live in the desert and, since I had recently returned from the Sonoran Desert in Arizona, I brought pictures to show them. All but two of the students were ELLs. One student, Hanefah, had been learning English for about three years, and her oral communication skills were fairly well developed. Here is an example of my efforts to get to the meaning of what Hanefah was saying as I discussed the desert with this class.

Pat: Did you know that it's against the law in Arizona to chop down a saguaro cactus?

Marvin: Why?

Pat: Because the government is protecting the saguaro. It's a very important part of the desert vegetation. Arizona is one of the only states that have saguaro cactuses.

Josseline: Mexico does.

Pat: You're right, Mexico does, and some parts of California and New Mexico. But Arizona has tons of them. If you have one in your yard and you don't want it, you can pay to have it moved, but you can't chop it down.

Mohammad: Is this one dead? (*He's pointing to a picture of a saguaro that is being passed around.*)

Pat: No, it's alive. But some birds have made holes in it to make their nests in there.

Avery: Oh yeah, we learned that. Remember, in that other book.

Hanefah: (*with a look of awe on her face*) They talk?

Pat: (*I am totally baffled by this question.*) What did you say, Hanefah?

Hanefah: I didn't know they can talk.

Pat: (*I quickly rewind a mental tape to think of what we last talked about.*) Do you mean the birds? The birds don't talk, Hanefah.

Hanefah: No, not birds, the trees.

Pat: No, the trees don't talk. What made you think that?

Hanefah: You said so.

Pat: I did? When? (*She doesn't answer.*) Hanefah, what did I say that made you think the trees could talk?

Hanefah: You said the tree was *alive.*

Pat: Ohhhh!

From there I was able to elaborate in order to clear up her misunderstanding. On first hearing this story you may think that Hanefah is not very bright, but you would be misinterpreting what actually happened in this exchange. It was Hanefah's misunderstanding of the meaning of the word *alive,* not her lack of intelligence that caused the problem. She *knew* trees don't talk; that's why she had a look of surprise on her face when she asked her question. Sometimes ELLs have a sense of a word, but in order to gain clarity of that word's meaning with all its connotations and nuances, they will need to be exposed to it in a variety of circumstances. To Hanefah, the word *alive* meant "things that talk." My explanation of the word with examples helped solidify a clearer sense of that word for her. Staying involved in conversation with the child long enough to discover a child's misunderstanding is important. Pay attention to comments an English language learner makes even when they seem off base. Listening in to their conversations with other children while at work or play and having real conversations with them can provide a wealth of knowledge.

In an article titled "The Gift of Attention" (2004/2005) Kathleen Fay and Suzanne Whaley comment on how hard many ELLs are working all day long to figure out what their teachers and classmates are saying. It seems only fair, they say, to meet English language learners halfway. I was trying to meet Hanefah halfway so that I could understand what she was thinking. Because I have a rapport with this student she was willing to continue to explore the problem with me. Without having a relationship with the student, many ELLs will shut down as you begin to probe. It's important that a child feel safe with you in order to keep the lines of communication open. "Negotiating meaning takes a lot of patience and humility on the part of both student and teacher. Our goal should be genuine two-way communication with English language learners" (p. 78).

Listening for the small things that second language learners say shows me how hard they are working to make sense of English. I remember when I was spending a lot of time doing interactive writing with Carla, a first-grade ELL who had been learning English since kindergarten. We would always chat for a little while and then, out of that conversation, Carla would decide what to write. She had been writing a lot about her cousin Juan.

On one particular day, however, she told me a story about her cousin Isabel. The story she decided to write was, "My cousin helped me. We made a birthday cake." She quickly wrote the word *my,* a known word. She was about to start writing the sounds in *cousin,* a word she had used to write about Juan for several days now, but she hesitated, looked up at me, and asked, "How do you say cousin *in girl?*" It took me a moment before it clicked with me what she was asking, but when I figured it out, I thought to myself, "What a brilliant child!" She knew that in Spanish there is a male and female word for *cousin* (*primo, prima*) just as there are gender endings for other words (*tio/tia, abuelo/abuela.*)

In English we often have different words to indicate male and female (*aunt/uncle* or *grandma/grandpa*), but we have only one word, *cousin,* which covers both genders. Carla's question told me that she was cognitively quite busy making generalizations about this new language she was learning. If we listen carefully, we can hear how smart our students are.

Developing a Classroom Community

Whenever I want to read examples of building communities in classrooms where ELLs are accepted, respected, and valued as unique individuals, I turn to Fay and Whaley's book *Becoming One Community: Reading and Writing with English Language Learners* (2004). Their essential points include: creating a safe environment, fostering trust, letting children talk, becoming a close observer of students, and opening new doors for learning. The underlying theme of their entire book is the respect that is awarded each child, no matter what their background, ability, or language level is. The stories they tell of teachers working with English language learners inspire me to become a better teacher for all the immigrant children I teach.

How does a teacher go about teaching respect for all members of the class, especially in a room where so few of the students are native English speakers? Emelie Parker, a kindergarten teacher, is an excellent example. Emelie doesn't just talk *to* her students with "line up" or "come to the rug" or "take out your writing folders." She talks *with* them all day long. One day I observed her listening to a kindergartner fairly new to English. Emelie had asked for predictions of what would happen next in a book. Her face was so intently focused on that student, you would have thought the child was telling her the meaning of life!

When other children tried to answer for the hesitant child or interrupt with their own ideas, Emelie gently put up her hand, never taking her eyes off the speaker. In this way, she modeled for the other children how to give respect to a fellow student who is speaking. Emelie let the child talk all around her idea, something ELLs often do when they can't find the words they need to express what they are trying to say. Patience and determination are often needed. Emelie responded with honest interest as well as vocabulary to support the child's thinking. In this brief moment Emelie illustrated to all her students that everyone has ideas to share in whatever way they can, no matter how much English they have. Being an attentive listener is the first step in teaching respect.

As you build classroom community, getting routines in place early in the year is helpful for all children, but especially for ELLs. In their book *"The Words Came Down!" English Language Learners Read, Write, and Talk Across the Curriculum, K–2,* Parker and Pardini write,

> We model activities clearly so that our ELLs know what is expected during each activity, during transitions, and during cleanup. These clear and consistent expectations are especially important to provide a degree of predictability throughout the day for second language learners. They are confronted with so much that is new that any standard routine must offer a degree of security. (2006, p. 92)

Helping ELLs feel safe and successful from the moment they arrive in their new school environment is a top priority for these authors. Their book gives multiple examples of how to create such opportunities not only in reading and writing workshops, but also in the content areas of math, science, and social studies.

Organizing for Instruction

Many professional books explicitly describe a classroom environment whose organization is based on a balanced literacy approach (see Chapter 2). In *Balancing Reading and Language Learning: A Resource for Teaching English Language Learners, K–5* (2005), Mary Cappellini illustrates how a program of "reading to, with, and by" and "writing to, with, and by" is especially beneficial for ELLs. Cappellini speaks from experience; she used such a program with her class of thirty-five first graders, all of whom were ELLs and half of whom were new to the school.

Organizing your classroom to allow for whole-group, small-group, and individual work provides an extremely supportive environment for ELLs. In whole-group lessons, they are exposed to many new strategies; in small groups, they can have lessons repeated with materials appropriately matched to their level and geared toward their strengths; and in individual time, they can receive specific scaffolding as the teacher zeros in on their needs.

Of all the contexts that make up strong reading and writing workshops, reading aloud and shared reading are two that are easy to use as springboards into oral language opportunities. During a read-aloud, the teacher can provide stopping points where children turn and talk to a partner in order to predict, make a connection, or comment about the text. Similarly, in shared reading, while reading together in a text large enough for all to see, the ELLs join in to whatever extent they feel comfortable. Shared reading also provides opportunities for questions, predictions, or comments about the print, pictures, or story line. After a read-aloud or a shared reading experience, teachers can encourage students to use drama or art to extend the story's meaning. During these times there's lots of talk as the students decide what to put in their mural, how to design their puppet, or what to write as they create a skit. It was during one of those extended activities (a reenactment of a picture book) that I learned never to underestimate an English language learner.

I read the book *Owl Babies* (1986) by Martin Waddell in two different first-grade classrooms. The students loved the story about the three little owls who were so frightened when their mother left them. They asked to have it read a second time and, of course, I obliged. On the second reading, the students chimed in every time the youngest owl said, "I want my mommy." In the story the three owls gather close on one branch, waiting anxiously for their mother's return. When she arrives they jump up and down with excitement and the Mother Owl says, "What's all the fuss? You knew I'd come back."

When I do reenactments with children I don't read from the book, but rather retell the story in my own words and let the children make up what the characters might say. In the first classroom, when I got to the part of the mother owl's return, I said, "and the baby owls were so excited they were jumping up and down." (When I pause, the students playing the baby owls jump around, look excited, and call out, "Hooray!" and other shouts of joy.) I continue with, "And the mother owl looked at them and said . . ." (I let my voice trail off to let Lizbeth, an ELL playing the Mother Owl's role, know it was her turn to make something up). Lizbeth jumped right in with, "What's all this racket?" In a second classroom, when I tried it out again, Jhomara, another ELL, said, "What's all the commotion?"

In both classrooms, the child chosen to play the mother's part had only begun learning English in kindergarten. I would never have guessed that either of those children knew the words *racket* or *commotion*. Not only did they come up with the phrase on their own, but they used it appropriately. This experience assures me that:

- Even when we are not directly instructing children in English, they are picking up vocabulary, common phrases, and novel sentence structures. (I wondered which teacher had used those expressions last year!)
- Choosing good literature to read aloud or Big Books for shared reading can engage children and serve as a springboard for other oral language activities.
- Using the creative arts—reenactments of stories, retellings with puppets, creating murals, class books, or wall stories—presents a perfect opportunity for oral language practice. Creative arts give kids a chance to use new language skills and vocabulary in various contexts. We see and hear things that might not otherwise surface.

Texts to Use with English Language Learners

In the book *Kids Come in All Languages: Reading Instruction for ESL Students,* V. G. Allen's chapter, "Selecting Materials for the Reading Instruction of ESL Children," suggests we use:

- books with predictable features;
- concept books;
- texts with illustrations that support and extend meaning;
- books that invite talk;
- ones that offer a framework for writing;
- ones that support the curriculum;
- and books that link to the students' cultures (1994, pp. 118–24).

Notice that the author does not suggest using decodable texts. Some early decodable texts focus so heavily on including words with the same sound that the meaning of the text and sometimes the structure of the English suffers. Controlled vocabulary books restrict the words children are exposed to in print. Story lines are pared down to telling what happened by using only a handful of high-frequency words and other words that follow a particular phonics rule. ELLs need something meaningful to read, just as other children do. We shouldn't dumb down the texts we use with ELLs, but rather keep the books rich in language structures and meaning. We want the children to hear English vocabulary and phrases used in a variety of ways.

When choosing a book for an ELL reading at an emergent level, be careful not to assume that a book with fewer words is automatically better. Sometimes a book with a minimal number of words is actually more difficult for the ELL because almost all the words are new vocabulary. For example:

Page 1   I like swings,
Page 2   and slides,
Page 3   and merry-go-rounds,
Page 4   and teeter-totters,
Page 5   and monkey bars.

Even though the pictures would support the vocabulary, all the words might be new English labels for the ELL. A book designed with the same words and pictures, but with a complete English language structure on each page, would benefit a child more, as in this example:

Page 1   I like to play on the swings.
Page 2   I like to play on the slide.
Page 3   I like to play on the merry-go-round.

The repetition of a common English language structure in this example supports the child's oral language development. The former example would only overwhelm the child with memorization of new English labels.

In Chapter 6 I discuss ideas for making books for early readers. Those examples would also help teachers who are at a loss for materials to use with their ELLs. Recently, several second- and third-grade teachers I work with have been experimenting with making books for their brand-new ELLs, just arrived from other countries. We are finding that these books are very helpful in:

- supporting beginning language structures;
- reinforcing high-frequency words within the context of meaningful text;
- building vocabulary;
- encouraging the earliest self-monitoring behaviors by the student;
- building reciprocity between reading and writing;
- adding to the motivation for reading during individual book-box time.

Assessing English Language Learners

All the professional texts mentioned in this chapter offer information about assessing English language learners—information about assessment tools for their developing language levels as well as ongoing assessment information about their reading and writing abilities. Each text supports the idea that observing ELLs *as they are engaged in the process of real reading and writing* will yield far more information than formal testing. "Simply put, test scores do not provide enough information to help teachers plan their instruction effectively. To plan instruction, teachers need to know how students are approaching, interpreting, and engaging in authentic literacy tasks" (Garcia 1994, p. 181).

I agree with this philosophy and try to illustrate it in my framework. The *here's what* phase is a time to find out what the child can do, can almost do, and cannot do as a reader while the child is engaged in the process of reading. The *then what* phase is also a time to observe carefully to see if the child is using the strategies and behaviors on his own without prompting from the teacher. Independence is always the goal. See Chapter 8 for a full discussion of assessment techniques and the connection between assessment and instruction.

The Rise in Number of English Language Learners

This chapter touches only briefly on the broad topics that relate to teaching English language learners—becoming a good listener; developing classroom community; organizing the classroom for whole-group, small-group, and individual learning; and closely assessing ELLs in authentic situations. I bow to the other experts who have written extensively about English language learners and hope teachers will take the time to investigate these topics further.

In today's world all teachers, not just the ELL teachers in a school, need to have expertise in supporting English language learners. According to recent studies reported in *Reading Today,* the number of ELLs in our schools is steadily increasing. That report states,

- Currently, 20 percent of U.S. students live in homes where a language other than English is spoken.
- By 2015 the percentage of K–12 students who will not have English as a first language will be 55 percent.

- Out of almost 3 million teachers surveyed by the U.S. National Center for Education Statistics, 41 percent report having ELLs in their classroom, but only 12.5 percent have received eight or more hours of ELL training (2004, p. 34).

Based on the statistics, it's clear that every elementary school teacher should receive training on teaching reading to ELLs. And it is my belief that training needs to extend much further than general background information. Classroom teachers need specific ways to introduce books to those students as well as ways to scaffold English language learners as they are engaged in the reading process. My hope is that this chapter will expand classroom teachers' awareness and knowledge base when teaching English language learners.

# In Brief

- There is no one definition or type that fits all English language learners.
- Being an ELL doesn't necessarily make that child a struggling reader.
- Teachers need to remain aware of a variety of aspects of the English language that can confuse ELLs so that they can build support for the child in the book introduction.
- Several ways to support ELLs so that they may be successful on the first reading of a text include: using explicit examples, letting children practice awkward language structures before reading, giving examples both in and out of the text, and providing a visual way to help the child read the word or phrase correctly on his own.
- Tuning in to what an ELL is saying and being a supportive listener is good practice.
- ELLs function well in environments that feel safe to them.
- A balanced literacy approach supports ELLs as they are learning to read and write.
- Reading aloud and shared reading are excellent opportunities for providing ELLs with oral language practice.
- Reading assessment of ELLs is best done during the context of real reading, just as it would be with native English speakers.

CHAPTER 8

Assessment— Finding Out What Each Struggling Reader Needs

Instruction for a struggling reader needs to be as tailored toward that child's specific needs as possible in order for teaching to be effective for that child. Readers who struggle are having problems putting together a system of strategies to help them understand text and solve words. Therefore it is the teacher's job to teach in ways that foster the acquisition of such a reading process system. For this to happen, assessment and instruction, as well as a philosophy of how children learn to read, must be closely aligned.

In this chapter I address two ways to acquire detailed information on a struggling reader's processing abilities: running records and individualized reading conferences. Both of these tools can be seamlessly woven into an established reading workshop. My focus is to help teachers analyze what they see and hear so that they can then plan instruction using that information. Included in the chapter are examples of teachers taking information from one or several children to develop curriculum for whole-class or small-group lessons. And finally, I show how teachers use "on-the-spot" assessment and instruction to clear up students' comprehension difficulties and confusions.

The Need for Ongoing Assessment

If I believe that readers construct a network of strategies for themselves, then my assessment should uncover the strategies the child uses or neglects to use, and my instruction should be founded on these discoveries. Looking at my framework for working with struggling readers, the bulk of my assessment takes place during the *here's what* stage, when I am trying to find out as much as I can about a reader, but assessment continues to play a role in the other parts of the framework. In the *so what* stage, I reflect on my assessment data to plan for instruction. As I begin teaching, in the *now what* phase, I am constantly weaving up and down the range of teaching actions based on what the child does or doesn't do. This on-the-spot assessment becomes part of my responsive teaching. Finally, in the *then what* stage, I am assessing to see if the child took on the strategy or behavior that I taught. Assessment remains *ongoing* and continually informs my instruction.

Ongoing assessment helps the teacher stay on top of what a particular struggling reader needs at a given time. It is done while the child is engaged in reading a text and can be an integral part of the daily reading workshop. Teachers who make assessment part of their daily classroom practices are in the best position to help struggling readers. "In a classroom that uses assessment to support learning, the divide between instruction and assessment blurs" (Leahy et al. 2005).

I've chosen running records and individualized reading conferences because these two assessment tools help me find answers to many questions:

- What does the child do when he gets stuck?
- What strategies or behaviors can she use on her own without teacher prompting?
- Does the child make several attempts before appealing to the teacher?
- What kinds of errors does the child make and why does he make them? Which errors is he able to self-correct?
- Is there a pattern in the way she goes about solving unknown words?
- Does he read for meaning?
- Does she stop when meaning breaks down?
- What does he do when he doesn't understand what he is reading?
- Does the student read fluently and well phrased or in a word-by-word manner?
- Does the child exhibit inefficient habits, such as an overdependence on only one way of figuring out words, which gets in the way of smooth processing of text?

Learning how to assess a child in this way takes time and practice, but all teachers can learn how to monitor, analyze, and interpret what a child does as he reads and then use that information for instruction.

Running Records—Definition and Purposes

For detailed instructions on taking and calculating running records, see the following publications:

Clay, Marie M. 1993a. *An Observation Survey of Early Literacy Achievement.* Portsmouth, NH: Heinemann.

Johnston, Peter. 2000. *Running Records: A Self-Tutoring Guide.* Portland, ME: Stenhouse.

Fountas, Irene C., and Gay Su Pinnell. 1996. *Guided Reading: Good First Teaching for All Children.* Portsmouth, NH: Heinemann.

Schulman, Mary, and Carleen Payne. 2000. *Guided Reading: Making It Work.* New York: Scholastic.

A running record is a tool created by Marie Clay and used by educators to document a child's reading of a text. The coding system enables teachers to produce a graphic representation of the student's reading. The codes are standardized; thus several teachers taking the same running record would produce the same result. This standardization also makes it possible to duplicate a fairly precise rendition of what the child did as he read the text.

A complete explanation of the mechanics of taking running records is beyond the scope of this book. To develop fluency with the taking of running records, a teacher needs training and practice. Once learned, this tool can be a quick and practical way to attain an enormous amount of information on that child's abilities. Fountas and Pinnell write that learning to take and analyze running records "sharpens a teacher's observational power and understanding of reading process" (1996, p. 89). I will assume that most teachers reading this text have basic familiarity with running records.

Teachers use the detailed accounts of running records:

- to graphically capture a child's reading behaviors, which can later be analyzed;
- to make plans for specific instruction based on a child's needs;
- to look for patterns in the child's way of responding across several running records;
- to decide on appropriate levels of texts for student instruction;
- to make decisions about grouping children;
- to provide information to other teachers who also work with the child or to parents;

♦ to keep a record of how the child is changing over time as he adds to his repertoire of strategies.

Helpful Hints Concerning Running Records

The following list may help clear up some common questions that often arise concerning running record use.

1. For classroom use, the ideal running record is taken the *second time* the child reads the book. The child has already been introduced to the text and the teacher has provided support during the first reading.

2. The teacher *does not prompt or teach* during the running record. She can say, "Try that again" or give the child the word if enough wait time has gone by.

3. *Accuracy rates* indicate whether the chosen text was appropriate for this child.

   ♦ 90–94 percent   instructional level   the child can use his system of strategies effectively

   ♦ 89 percent or lower   frustration level   often too difficult for the child to use his network of strategies effectively

   ♦ 95–100 percent   easy level   the child can handle more challenges in texts

4. *Self-correction (SC) rates* show the proportion of errors the child corrected in relation to the total number of errors the child made. Scores of 1:2, 1:3, 1:4 are usually considered good rates while higher than 1:5 might be cause for concern.

5. The teacher often picks a *teaching point after* the running record is completed. Examples: reinforcing a strategy or behavior the child used, supporting the child in correcting an error, focusing on a section to encourage better fluency, and so on.

6. Running records are used mostly on readers who read *emergent, progressing, transitional,* and *developing levels.* For lengthy books, a passage of 100 to 200 words will suffice.

7. For students who read on *independent through fluent levels,* an individualized reading conference is more applicable. However, teachers who

have knowledge of running records will find it easier to observe and infer strategy use during the reading conference.

The accuracy and self-correction rates give us some information about the child's reading, but further analysis is necessary. Scores alone don't tell the whole story. In fact, two children can receive the same accuracy scores and have the same SC rate and yet be totally different in how they approach text, how they attempt to solve problems, or what they neglect to use (Morrison 1994). Each child would need different instruction. Learning to read running records involves much more than learning to calculate scores, as you will see in the analysis section.

Running Record Analysis

Before I was trained in Reading Recovery ten years ago, I often sat in awe watching excellent Reading Recovery teachers pick a teaching point after taking a running record. They seemed able to quickly assess what it was the child needed to learn at that moment in time. I wondered, "How did they know that so quickly? What were they seeing in the running record that I evidently wasn't able to see?" Over the years I have improved my ability to analyze running records, to look for patterns in the way the child solves problems, and to hypothesize about a child's processing, which has led me to teach in ways that support a child's strategy use. But because I can remember when I wasn't able to do this very well, I make it a goal to support other teachers in acquiring this knowledge.

When analyzing running records, a teacher's perspective needs to be *strategy based* rather than *item based*. She is looking not only at items such as words missed or letter sounds confused, but also at the operations or actions the child tried as he attempted to figure out words and confirm his reading. Peter Johnston says that running records are only "an estimate of a child's processing" (2000, p. 1). One can never know exactly what goes on in the head of a child as he reads. But by examining what the child did or neglected to do, we can infer the strategies he used. The behaviors we see, hear, and notice help us hypothesize about the child's processing.

I noticed a few years ago that even though many of the teachers I was working with knew how to take running records and calculate scores, very few reported using them to drive their instruction. The missing piece seemed to be the analysis. When I began making time to support teachers' running record analysis skills, they experienced a positive shift in their assessing abilities, grew in understanding of the reading process, and used assessment data more effectively when teaching struggling readers.

To help teachers new to analyzing, I have them discuss with partners this question: "What might you see on a running record if you thought a child was using the following strategies?"

predicting
searching and gathering
self-monitoring
using visual information effectively
using a balance of sources of information
making multiple attempts

It's important for teachers to first express their understandings of each of these terms and what each might sound like when a child is reading a text. Then we discuss possible instances, using examples.

Reading a Running Record for Strategies and Reading Process

Predicting   A child who is predicting substitutes a known word for an unknown word rather than waiting for someone to give him the word. For example,

Child:	pants	ground	like	talk	sit
Text:	trousers	grass	look	take	stay

Sometimes the child predicts with meaning and structural information, like *pants* for *trousers,* a word that makes sense and sounds right in the sentence. At other times he uses not only meaning and structural cues, but also checks some of the letters, like *ground* for *grass.* When a child substitutes a word that looks similar to the word in the text but doesn't really make sense, like *talk* for *take,* we could say he is predicting with visual information, just using some of the letters, but not cross-checking with meaningful sources of information.

I look for patterns in the kinds of substitutions a child makes. Then I plan my teaching based on the source of information he is neglecting to use. Or, if I find that the child does not predict at all, then that is where my teaching begins.

Searching and Gathering If a child is searching for more information to help him solve an unknown word, you might see examples like the following on his running records:

● *Rereadings.* Sometimes a child returns to the beginning of a sentence to gather meaningful information, thus putting the story or text ideas back in his head.

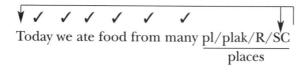

(Note: The text is not usually shown on the running record but I have included it in these examples for the ease of the reader.)

● *Reading on.* A student might read past a word to help her gather meaning from the rest of the sentence in order to solve an unknown word.

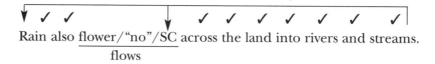

Sometimes the child doesn't do this orally and, therefore, it would not be coded on the running record. However, a teacher may notice the child looking past the unknown word and mouthing the words.

● *Searching the pictures.* This, too, is evidence that the child is actively searching for information to help himself. Though this behavior is not coded on a running record, the teacher is sitting right beside the child during the record taking, and may observe the child glancing at the illustration on the page.

● *Searching the letters.*

k/can/and/✓	b ar/ing/bark/✓
candy	barking

In these examples the child is looking for letters or chunks she recognizes. She may be linking to other words she knows that contain this sound. The check mark indicates that she finally solved the word.

● *Gathering information from prior knowledge.* Sometimes during a running record a child verbalizes some of his thinking. Examples of what a child might say are: "I have that word in my other book" or "I know what it is, but I can't say it. My cousin has one of those." There is no code for this, but a teacher can choose to make a notation on the record if the child says something to indicate that he is using his schema to figure out a word.

If a child does not use any searching or gathering behaviors, then your instruction can focus on teaching him how. Readers need to actively search for information that helps them figure out words.

Self-Monitoring   Self-monitoring means that the child is checking and confirming that what he is reading makes sense, sounds right, and looks right. Therefore, any time you see an indication of the child stopping to attempt to work something out, you could infer that the student is monitoring his reading. He may not always be able to fix the error, but he is still monitoring that something is not quite right.

$$\frac{\text{scared/fraid /A}}{\text{frightened /T}} \qquad \begin{array}{l}\text{A = Appeals for help} \\ \text{T = Teacher told the word}\end{array}$$

A self-correction would automatically indicate that a child was self-monitoring. The child made an error, felt the mismatch, and so he stopped and fixed it.

✓ ✓ ✓ ✓   ✓ ✓   ✓ ✓
Next to his bike was a $\underline{\text{bike/SC}}$ new bike.
                              brand

In another instance the child may reread to fix his intonation because of a punctuation cue. For example, the child may have read the words first in a monotone voice, but then reread to make it sound more expressive.

▼✓   ✓ ✓
Help! I'm stuck/R

Though it would be coded only as a rereading on the running record, the teacher could note that the child seemed to be self-monitoring for punctuation cues.

One way that *lack of self-monitoring* would show up on a running record would be a substitution that makes no sense and yet the child continues on. For example,

✓ ✓ ✓ ✓   ✓

Rusty ran away. Come <u>book</u> Rusty.

                    back

Using Visual Information Effectively

<u>in/sss/✓</u>	<u>sh sh/look/sh ook/SC</u>	<u>b/buck/SC</u>
inside	shook	back

Notice in the above examples that the child is searching for part of the word—the letters, sounds, and chunks he knows—to help him take that word apart phonetically. When analyzing running records, I notice when the child is using visual information *effectively* as opposed to when he might make random sounds and never get close to the word. In the last example, you can see how the child came close enough to the correct pronunciation that meaning probably supported him as he finally solved the word. If you notice that a child is not using visual information effectively, then your teaching needs to focus on this.

Using a Balance of Sources of Information   When teachers learn about running records, their training usually includes the first level of analysis—how to circle M, S, or V (representing meaning, structure, or visual information) in the error and self-correction columns. The circling is a way to code the teacher's thinking. She is inferring why she thinks the child made the error and why he might have fixed it. The recordings help show examples of what you might see when a child is using a balance of all three sources of information. Sometimes the error itself shows that the child was using all three sources of information even though he read the word incorrectly, as in this example:

	E	SC	E	SC
<u>surprised</u>	1		Ⓜ Ⓢ Ⓥ	
startled				

At other times the child makes a meaningful error and then fixes it with visual information, like this:

	E	SC	E	SC
<u>walked/SC</u>		1	Ⓜ Ⓢ V	M S Ⓥ
strolled				

Or he makes the error because of initially using visual and structural information, but then fixes it with meaning. For example,

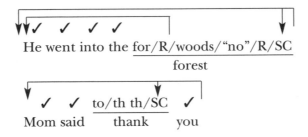

Making Multiple Attempts When a reader becomes stuck on a word, he sometimes tries several different things to figure out the word—sounding the letters, reading on, rereading, putting in a meaningful substitution, and so on. On a running record, you might see examples like these:

He went into the for/R/woods/"no"/R/SC
                 forest

Mom said   to/th th/SC   you
            thank

Whether or not the child is successful in solving the word is not what we're observing here. We're looking to see what strategies she's using and if she is flexible in her strategy use.

In the same way that an emergent reader learns to "look at print and make sense of it," teachers can learn to "look at running records and make sense of the child's processing." When teachers learn to "see" the strategies in a running record, they take on a whole new view of assessment. They deepen their understanding of how a reader's network of strategies (see Figure 2–2) connects with assessment and instruction. I have seen many teachers experience an "aha" moment after discussions such as these around running records.

The Power Behind Examining Self-Corrections

Self-corrections provide a very specific lens on a child's reading process. They are "signals that reading work is being done" (Clay 2001). Self-corrections help us see what the child *can do;* they are indications of problem solving in action. The child makes an error, experiences the dissonance that the error causes, stops, returns to the error searching for other information, works it out, and successfully fixes his mistake. We need to congratulate that effort as a way to reinforce the processing the child used to solve the problem.

Sometimes teachers tend to give too much attention to accuracy, which only leads them to overemphasize the child's errors. On the contrary, when you study self-corrections you are examining solutions, not errors. The solutions that the child uses to fix the error can be strengthened by using your instructional time to reinforce them.

What are the benefits of focusing on the child's self-corrections as part of your teaching?

1. When you bring the child's attention to a self-correction you are reinforcing the process by which he did the solving. You want the child thinking, "Yeah, you're right, I really did do that and it worked for me. Maybe I'll try that same thing again sometime."
2. When you focus on a self-correction you are focusing on a child's success. And we all know that success breeds more success; it adds to self-esteem and supports future motivation. The child is gaining intrinsic rewards for the reading work he's done. He might be thinking, "That wasn't so hard. I did it all by myself. I'm getting pretty good at this stuff." He may be more willing to take risks and try again on another day, another text.
3. After going over a self-correction with the teacher, the child may be more willing to go to a place in the text where he made an error that he wasn't able to fix and try again.
4. Self-corrections also provide excellent opportunities for self-instruction (Clay 2001, p. 205). Even without teacher intervention the child can learn things from them on his own. When a child fixes a word, he not only receives confirmation on the *word* itself (so that he will perhaps recognize the word in the future), but the *process* by which he did the solving of that word is also confirmed.

Clay writes that self-corrections are "self-congratulatory" (2001, p. 204). This idea reminds me of a video I once saw. Esther, an emergent reader, had been working with a teacher for several days on "checking the first letter and getting your mouth ready for a tricky word." The video shows the teacher taking a running record on Esther. At one point Esther is almost ready to quit on a word, showing facial signs of frustration, but then she tries the first letter, goes back and rereads, and successfully solves the word. Immediately, Esther looks up at the teacher and says, "There, I fixed it!" with a delightful smile on her face. Her comment was her way of patting herself on the back!

Viewing running records together with colleagues helps teachers learn to analyze the information and use it for instructional purposes. Discussions around what you see in the records and what that might mean for your next teaching interaction with this child are worthwhile learning sessions. In the hands of an informed teacher who knows how to analyze the data, running records can be a powerful assessment tool for teaching struggling readers.

Districts may provide training on the coding methods and scoring of running records, but often run out of the time or money to provide staff development on in-depth analysis of running records. Whenever possible, literacy teams, administrators, or reading teachers should find ways to provide this type of staff development at school sites. It has been my experience that you will see improvement in teachers' understandings of the reading process and they will become better equipped to match assessment and instruction for struggling readers.

Individual Reading Conferences

Many teachers who are not trained in taking running records can still quite capably observe a child's network of strategies. Some upper-grade teachers and I meet regularly with students to confer about the books the students are reading. We meet more often with struggling readers and less often with readers who are reading above grade level.

During an individualized reading conference the teacher sits beside a child who is reading a book. The text may be one the child has recently been introduced to in a guided reading session or it may be a self-selected text. The child reads aloud a few pages and we make notations about what we infer about his strategy use. Rather than ask a series of questions, we converse with the child about the text and pick up information about whether he was able to comprehend what he read.

In her book *More Than Guided Reading* (2005), Cathy Mere talks about how she uses individual conferences not only for assessment, but also to do some immediate teaching. She warns us that one conference will not necessarily change a student as a reader, but that many conferences over time can. Mere reassures us that we will all get better at making assessment decisions and teaching one-on-one. She writes, "There is no guarantee that I will always make the right move or provide the ideal words of advice. I try to remember that it is the power of these conferences over time that will make a difference" (p. 59).

For recording the data from individualized conferences, some teachers use anecdotal note taking or checklists. I suggest the form in Appendix A, which my colleague Terri Smith developed with me. This form is designed to help teachers think about a child's processing. It provides a way to listen with an eye and ear for strategies. The reflection note after each section is intended to support teachers in making decisions about the child's strategy use, fluency, or comprehension.

In section one, the teacher puts a check mark next to each item that she notices the child doing when stuck. Section two is for recording the substitutions the child makes while reading. If the child self-corrects, the teacher can add SC. In section three, the teacher records how she feels the child was reading in relation to fluency—well paced and with appropriate phrasing or choppily. She might also make note of which punctuation cues the child attended to or neglected, his intonations, or his expression while reading. Section four includes a retelling piece to help the teacher gather basic comprehension information. (The next section elaborates on digging for more detailed comprehension information.) Section five is for any other observations. I sometimes use this section to discover whether the child is able to use the strategy discussed in whole-class or small-group lessons. For example, if the teacher recently did a lesson on context clues, she might ask the child about a particular vocabulary word in the text to see what he would do to figure out its meaning.

This form offers guidelines about what to listen for as you are sitting beside a child. You can adapt it and make it more workable for your own personal note-taking style.

Digging Deeper—Assessing the Cause of Comprehension Confusion

What if we thought about comprehension as existing on a continuum, with one end being *total lack of comprehension* and the other end *complete comprehension?* It would be easy to place a child on either end of this continuum. For example, a child who totally understands everything he reads can probably convince you of that with his inferences, connections, and comments about the text. On the other end of the continuum, you can usually get a good sense when a child doesn't understand anything of what he read, totally lacking comprehension. Anywhere in between, things begin to get murky. You may feel the child didn't quite understand, but you may be unsure why he's getting confused. It is during the reading conference conversation that I try to determine exactly *why* a student is not constructing meaning. The only way I can teach him how to get unstuck is to figure out what caused him to get stuck!

The more teachers become acquainted with the reasons why some struggling readers become confused and stop comprehending, the better equipped they are to plan instruction for those students. Some of the ideas in the following list are adapted from the work of Cris Tovani (2000) and Franki Sibberson and Karen Syzmusiak (2003).

Upper-elementary readers who struggle often get stuck in their reading because they

- lack fluency and proper pacing; are unable to use the punctuation to help them comprehend the text
- can read the words, but don't know what some of them mean
- have trouble decoding multisyllabic words
- fail to recognize when the setting changes
- lose track of the characters
- do not self-monitor for meaning; read right past words or phrases that make no sense
- fail to notice who or what a pronoun is referring to
- daydream while reading; get to the bottom of the page not knowing what they just read
- do not pick up author clues about who the narrator of the story is
- get confused by the format or structure of the text
- do not take advantage of text features to aid comprehension when reading nonfiction
- are unable to infer beyond the literal meaning of the text
- do not use a repertoire of strategies as meaning begins to break down; don't try to visualize, make connections, paraphrase, or ask questions to help themselves stay engaged with text.

You may want to use the following activity at a grade-level meeting or with any group of teachers who want to improve their teaching for comprehension with struggling readers.

1. Teachers pair up and each set of teachers picks one problem from the list.
2. Each pair then brainstorms how they would develop a lesson to alleviate the problem they selected.
3. The teacher pairs share ideas.
4. Each teacher then picks one lesson that they would like to try with their class or a small group of students.
5. Teachers plan a time to come back and share what happened with the lesson.

When I narrow down the possibilities of why this child is getting confused, I have a better chance of actually teaching him ways to fix his comprehension. Many of the lessons included in this book address these reading comprehension issues.

Assessment of Individual Students Leading to Whole-Class Lessons

Sitting next to a child as he is reading a text is sometimes the only way to decipher what the root of his comprehension problem is. Once you determine the cause of the student's breakdown in meaning, you could teach him a way to help himself when a similar comprehension problem arises. This explicit modeling with a gradual release of responsibility supports the child as he learns to self-initiate the strategy or behavior on his own.

The teaching focus you decide on for one student can lead you to develop whole-class or small-group lessons to benefit other students in your class. For example, while working with Benjy, a fourth-grade struggling reader, I noticed how his lack of attention to punctuation caused him to misinterpret information in a book on sharks.

Benjy: (*reading the words correctly, but with poor fluency and lack of attention to punctuation*) "When a shark loses a tooth, a new one grows in its place. In one year, a tiger shark can lose 2,400 teeth!"

Pat: Wow! That's pretty interesting. Tell me something you learned in this part.

Benjy: They lose their teeth sometimes. And it takes a year for one to grow.

Pat: A whole year? That seems like a long time to grow a tooth. Show me where it says that.

Benjy: (*reads with his finger under these words*) "A new one grows in its place in one year."

Benjy was running words together and passing periods, and that changed the meaning for him. I immediately focused on teaching him to read the periods and commas correctly.

When I met with the classroom teacher and told her the story of this particular interaction, she said, "Oh, I've got five or six kids who do that all the time!" We met that afternoon to discuss ways she could introduce whole-class and small-group lessons on "reading the punctuation to aid your comprehension." When we assess a problem with our students we need to focus our instruction on ways to solve the problem.

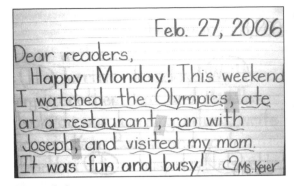

Figure 8–1
Dear Readers, February 27

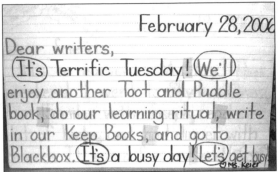

Figure 8–2
Dear Writers, February 28

Another time I was working with Bryn, a second grader who was a struggling reader at the beginning of the school year, but was making exceptional progress by March. She was reading this line in a Henry and Mudge book: "Mudge wagged his tail, rolled over, and snored." I noticed that her fluency was slightly off and I was not quite sure she comprehended what just happened in the story. I determined that she didn't know how to correctly read *commas in a series*. I helped her with some on-the-spot teaching, but then informed her teacher that she may want to include some sentences with *commas in a series* in her next few morning messages. We discussed how this concept might help some students not only in their reading but also in their writing (see Figures 8–1 and 8–2).

During those morning message experiences the teacher let Bryn help teach the other students. After the class studied this print convention for a few days, the teacher shared a funny incident with me. She was telling the children to line up for lunch: "Please put your writing folders away, push in your chairs, and quietly line up." Bryn called out, "Hey, if you write that down, that would need lots of commas. It's a series." If your instruction is clear and provides lots of opportunity for practice, children will internalize what you are teaching them to do.

Making On-the-Spot Assessment Decisions

Assessment that you take during one interaction with a child can inform your planning for the next time you meet with that child. Analysis of running records or notes taken during individualized reading conferences or even during guided reading sessions feed our decisions of what a child needs to learn next. But sometimes you must change your plans midstream. Teachers need to remain flexible enough to switch gears if something comes up. You may notice while reading with a child something that needs to be addressed right away.

One day my plan for working with Diego, a third-grade ELL reading on an independent level, was to reinforce the use of context clues that the teacher and I had been working on with the whole class. Diego read these lines in a text: "After school, Bill sat down on the porch with Mom. He stroked his dog, Patches."

When he read this, his pronunciation of the word *stroked* was not quite clear and I suspected he didn't know what it meant. I asked him to use his context clues to see if he could put in another word that made sense. He chose *barked*. When I probed further, he said he picked *barked* because it was about the dog. My on-the-spot assessment told me that Diego was having trouble with pronoun referents. For an English language learner this was not unusual. Diego didn't realize that the word *he* was referring to Bill, not the dog. Without understanding this first, he would never be able to get to the meaning of the word *stroked*. I quickly shifted my teaching to focus on learning about pronoun referents.

Conclusion

The kind of assessment discussed throughout this chapter is very specific to the needs of struggling readers. I emphasize the analysis of running records and the careful examination of strategies and behaviors during individualized reading conferences because I find that those tools provide the best information for my instruction. There is, however, a much bigger picture of assessment for running a whole classroom filled with readers of all levels. Grades, standardized tests, grade-level checklists for reading or writing behaviors, numbers of words read correctly on word lists, or words spelled correctly on spelling inventories all contribute in some way to the larger assessment picture. Many teachers make use of these to inform parents or for keeping a general record of how students are doing.

Benchmarking assessment, like the Developmental Reading Assessment (DRA), can also be very helpful in planning what level text might be appropriate for each child and charting some beginning information on the child's strategy use. DRA testing also helps teachers with grouping practices early in the year. Benchmarking done at the end of the school year is often used to send general information to the next year's teacher.

For information on other assessment tools, ways to organize and manage your assessments, and checklists and surveys on children's interests and attitudes about reading, look at the following suggestions:

Schulman, M., and C. Payne. 2000. *Guided Reading: Making It Work*, Chapter 7.

Robb, L. 1998. *Easy-to-Manage Reading and Writing Conferences: Practical Ideas for Making Conferences Work*, Chapters 3–5.

Dorn, L., and C. Soffos. 2001. *Shaping Literate Minds: Developing Self-Regulated Learners*, Chapter 3.

Hindley, J. 1996. *In the Company of Children*, Chapters 9–10.

Routman, R. 2003. *Reading Essentials: The Specifics You Need to Teach Reading Well*, Chapters 6–7.

In Brief

- In order to assess a child's reading we must first understand how the reading process works.
- Assessment and instruction must be closely aligned for teaching to benefit struggling readers.
- Making time in your reading workshop to include running record taking or individualized reading conferences will benefit all students, especially struggling readers; ongoing assessment drives instruction.
- Running records, when used by an informed teacher who understands how to analyze them, can be a powerful assessment tool.
- Comprehension is difficult to assess, but conversations as part of individualized conferences can help teachers narrow down the cause of a child's confusion.
- Flexibility as you work with struggling readers is important so that you can teach toward what the child needs most at the time.
- Assessment of individual students can lead teachers to plan explicit lessons for the whole class or small groups of children.

CHAPTER 9

What Will It Take?

During the course of writing this book I would often take my work with me as I ate lunch at my favorite café. One Saturday, two teachers sitting at a table next to me noticed my pile of professional books and asked what I was working on. I told them I was writing a book for classroom teachers to help them with their struggling readers. They got excited and one asked, "In twenty-five words or less, could you tell me what to do for my third-grade struggling readers?" I just chuckled, hoping she'd realize I wasn't about to try to answer that question. But she pressed on. "I know you can't really do it that fast, but can you give me just a little something to do on Monday?" The desperation in her voice made me wish for a simple answer. I wanted more than anything to be able to help her. But there are no easy answers when it comes to helping struggling readers.

I'm not surprised by this teacher's hoping for a simple answer. The mind-set of the simple theory of reading is quite prevalent. I've seen it supported in ads for quick-fix phonics kits. I hear it in the speeches of politicians who believe that more tests, coupled with raised standards, will automatically lead to solving the problems of our lowest-level readers. I even see it in ads for teacher workshops. One ad recently claimed to be able *in one day* to help students reach their maximum potential; close the reading gap and rescue students who are falling through the cracks; improve all reading programs K–12; meet state and local standards; increase promotion rates; and reduce dropout rates. Wow! If all it takes is one day, then why haven't we been doing this all along?

If learning to read has a simple answer, then why do we still have so many students who struggle? The truth is that the process of reading is not *simple* at all, but rather very *complex*. And we all need to do our part to begin to change the simple theory mind-set—of teachers, parents, administrators, publishers of reading series, education directors in state and national positions, politicians, and society in general.

This chapter first addresses the differences between the simple and complex theories of reading and why it's important for all teachers working with struggling readers to understand the latter one. Then it discusses staff development opportunities to support teachers' learning about reading process, and, finally, leaves the reader with some closing thoughts on the topic of struggling readers.

The Simple Theory Versus the Complex Theory of Learning to Read

The simple theory, also called the item/skills-based theory (Clay 2001), considers reading to be a compilation of items and skills. Most supporters believe that when these items—letters, sounds, and sight vocabulary—are taught well and in some sequential order, the child will emerge as a reader. *But there is so much more happening in the head of a budding reader.* As a reader is learning phonics and building a sight vocabulary of easily recognizable words, he is also constructing ways to solve problems when he's stuck; self-monitor in order to confirm that what he is reading makes sense; and link his new discoveries with old knowledge. This composite of thinking abilities—figuring out, fixing up, linking, and monitoring for comprehension—is often referred to as a network of strategies. The complex theory of reading, also called a literacy-processing theory (Clay 2001), begins with an understanding of these strategies and the realization that the struggling reader is having trouble building a network of strategies on his own.

The simple theory of reading has often been enough for many children. My own daughters, now in their late twenties, learned from a skills-oriented series and spent their days in primary classrooms filling in many phonics workbook pages. Yet they knew that reading was supposed to make sense. If they became confused while reading, they stopped and solved the problem. They developed ways to detect when something was wrong, to fix up errors, and to maintain their fluency and comprehension. They did this, just as many other children do every day, without explicit instruction in strategy use. The construction of a network of strategies happens quite easily and naturally for children *as long as they are not struggling* (Clay 2001).

The fact that many children can learn to read no matter what program or materials are being used accounts for the widespread popularity of the simple theory of reading. Supporters think, "Many children have learned to read this way. If it works for some, then it should work for all."

But for struggling readers the process of reading doesn't fall into place naturally and easily. As I've shown repeatedly throughout this text, the struggling reader isn't independently putting together a complex network of strategies that will help him solve the print and understand the text. He is not figuring out ways to solve problems *on his own*. But we have also seen that the struggling reader *can* build a system of strategies if he has a teacher who:

- observes carefully to find out what he needs,
- explicitly models strategies and behaviors that proficient readers use,
- supports and scaffolds the student as he tries out what's been demonstrated,
- stays with him, lessening those supports little by little, and
- releases control as the student takes on the strategy or strategic behavior for himself.

All struggling readers need teachers who understand the complex process of reading. As an advocate for the work that needs to be done with struggling readers, I often say they need *more and better* of what we know is great teaching for all children. "Why more?" someone might ask. "That doesn't seem fair." My friend and colleague Ruth Powell always says, "Being fair doesn't mean every child gets everything the same. Being fair means every child gets what every child needs." And struggling readers need and deserve teachers who are willing to work harder, think harder, learn more, plan better, instruct well, and observe continually. They require teachers who will take the extra step to uncover their unique needs and design curriculum based on those findings.

Richard Allington, the 2005–2006 president of the International Reading Association, recently made his plea for high-quality instruction.

Struggling readers need larger amounts of more expert, more personalized, and more intensive reading instruction. In the end, the quality of that instruction is critical, and high-quality instruction for struggling readers cannot simply be boxed up and shipped to a site. High-quality, reading instruction, especially for struggling readers, requires the expertise to identify just where the reader has gotten off-track and then to design instruction that moves the reader back onto an accelerated track of development (2006, p. 20).

A Vision of What's Possible

I always enjoy listening to *This, I Believe,* a series on National Public Radio where people read their essays. The essays cover a range of topics and are written and read by people from all walks of life. The stories express hopes and dreams, personal philosophies, and the core beliefs that guide a person's life.

My hope and dream is that every child who is struggling with the process of learning to read will have a teacher with the knowledge, teaching techniques, and desire to teach her well. And I believe that such a world can exist. When I use the word *complex* I'm not suggesting that the task is so hard we won't be able to accomplish it. We can. We need teachers who are willing to continually grow in their understanding of what goes on in the head of a proficient reader so that they can observe, plan, and instruct struggling readers as each begins to build his repertoire of strategies. By learning to observe carefully through a strategic lens, teachers could discover the unique needs of each child. Teachers would make time for working with a struggling reader, build on each child's strengths, and use responsive teaching at every interaction with this student.

Is it possible for every teacher, specialist, administrator, volunteer, or teacher's aide who works with a struggling reader to achieve this understanding? It would take time and effort, but, yes, it is doable. *This, I believe.*

Teachers Learning Together

So how might each and every teacher who works with struggling readers gain this knowledge? Let's start with how teachers learn. There are a lot of similarities between the way adults learn and the way children learn. Teachers learn best when they do the following:

- Actively participate
- Are respected within the learning community
- Are provided with opportunities to observe new concepts in context
- Have time to discuss common concerns
- Feel safe and know they will be supported when they try something new
- Have shared responsibility for their own learning
- Are given time to absorb and reflect on new information (Lyons and Pinnell 2001)

When discussing how she works with staffs concerning literacy, a friend of mine always quips, "I won't do drive-bys." The way to help a staff grow in their literacy understandings is not through a one-shot workshop, but rather by learning together over time while they are involved in the process of teaching reading and writing to children.

In *Apprenticeship to Literacy* the authors write, "It takes many dedicated people working together to ensure every child's right to literacy. A single program or a single teacher cannot bring about comprehensive changes within the school. The importance of teachers working together as a team of educators whose goal is to support the total child cannot be underestimated" (Dorn, French, and Jones 1998, p. 155).

We have to help each other understand the complexity of the reading process. The school systems, individual schools, and literacy teams that are beginning to fill this need find ways for teachers to continue learning on the job. They provide ongoing staff development over time. The teachers in these buildings do the following:

- Think of themselves as constant learners
- Read and discuss professional literature
- Put their heads together to talk about issues concerning struggling readers
- Observe children carefully and ask others to observe them so that they can get input from many sources
- Converse about literacy—how it is acquired and how comprehension is best strengthened
- Constantly reflect on their own practice in the classroom to evaluate how best to help children learn to read

Many small groups of teachers in schools are coming together to direct their own learning. Donald Graves (2001) maintains that educators who establish relationships for working collaboratively on issues can be an important source of energy for teachers.

Ongoing Staff Development as a Possible Starting Point

Teachers don't have to learn about reading process and helping struggling readers in organized staff development formats that are *required* for all staff members. In fact, it's probably best to start with optional learning opportunities, for which interested teachers can sign up. The following are a few ways that the schools I've been associated with have tried to help teachers continue their learning.

- Teachers-as-readers—Many groups form around reading a professional book together. When someone gets a tip about a great book to read to improve classroom practice and increase student achievement, he puts out an e-mail to the staff and a discussion group inevitably takes shape. Usually the book is divided into three or four parts and teachers meet monthly or bimonthly to discuss the sections.
- Using resource persons in different ways—One year I worked with the first-grade teachers, eleven in all, on a long-term staff development project. I attended their hourlong weekly meetings, which the administrator had arranged to take place on school time. Half of each meeting was spent on professional development. I facilitated the discussions during that time on topics that the teachers suggested and that related to struggling readers.

  As a group we decided halfway through the year to make an assessment wall; students' names were posted according to the reading level on which they were being instructed in the classroom. (This suggestion came from the literacy coaching schools described in *Shaping Literate Minds* [Dorn and Soffos 2001], a text we were reading together.) We used a three-paneled posterboard, the type students often use for science fair projects. We could then fold it up since we didn't want the confidential information on permanent display. The boards helped us find a focus for our learning. For example, if we noticed a lot of children stuck at a particular level, we discussed ways to get those children moving. On occasion I brought in one of those children and modeled a lesson with that child in front of the teachers. Another time we used the boards to focus in on several struggling readers. We divided into teams of three teachers for each child. We all read with that child, took and analyzed a running record, and came back together to discuss plans for accelerating that child. We believed that the struggling readers in first grade belonged to all of us and we could all learn to become better teachers of reading by putting our heads together.

◆ Sharing expertise—Reading Recovery teachers in our building for years have been getting together with other first-grade teachers to discuss issues and share their expertise in working with readers who struggle. In fact, their twice-monthly discussion group is open to any interested faculty member, any grade level. Having Reading Recovery–trained teachers in your building can be an incredible asset if the staff wants to learn about the complex theory of reading process.

◆ Literacy Learning Groups (LLG)—For the past three years in my district I have facilitated a particular kind of study group. Each year we offered this long-term staff development opportunity to any interested Title I reading teacher. The Title I teacher could invite two classroom teachers from kindergarten through grade 2 to sign up with her for a series of eight sessions, all offered on school time. Teams from about fifteen Title I qualifying schools signed up each year. Title I funds were used to secure subs for these teachers when they attended the half-day sessions each month. The purpose of LLG was to delve in-depth into the complex theory of reading, to help teachers layer their understandings about reading process, and to expand teachers' knowledge and skills for teaching struggling readers. In between sessions, the Title I teacher worked collaboratively with the classroom teachers in their rooms at least an hour or two each week. All the participants agreed to complete readings from professional texts, try out the ideas from the sessions in their classrooms, watch each other teach, and meet periodically to continue the conversations begun in the sessions. Some teams even opted to include online dialogues about certain students or topics.

◆ Literacy Collaborative (LC) is taking hold in many districts and serves as an excellent model. This program is successful in part because the LC facilitator gets excellent training, spends time developing trust and mutual respect with the teachers she works with, teaches in a classroom for half her day, works side by side with teachers, and facilitates discussions around professional literature. Not every district can afford this model yet, but we can certainly learn from the LC example. Teachers learn best with the support of a more knowledgeable other while engaged in the context of teaching children to read and write.

- Using the framework *here's what/ so what/ now what/ then what*—One school year I worked with a team of teachers for one half-day per week. These second-through-fifth-grade teachers focused their learning on one struggling reader at a time. Using the framework described in this book, we assessed the child, reflected on the data, planned instruction together, and watched each other teach this child. We also chose to meet once a month after school to discuss related issues.

- Wednesday workshops—It has been a tradition at Bailey's Elementary School for new teachers to attend before-school sessions for thirty minutes on Wednesday mornings, before the children arrive. Here they are provided with extra on-the-job support for organizing and managing reading/writing workshops and for teaching reading to English language learners. Over the years the tradition has changed and taken on a different shape based on the needs of the staff. Now, different four-to-six-week sessions are given on a variety of topics, in all subject areas. All sessions are led by in-house experts. In language arts there might be a miniseries offered on "running record in-depth analysis" or "comprehension strategies." Though new teachers are required to attend a certain number of minicourses, the topics are also open to all staff members.

There are so many ways that teachers can learn and grow as teachers of reading. *Language Arts,* a journal from the National Council of Teachers of English (NCTE) devoted an entire issue filled with ideas about rethinking professional development (May 2005).

What's in a Name?

Though I use the terms *struggling reader* and *hardest-to-teach children* throughout this text, the terms cause a bit of discomfort for me. Labels like these seem to have such negative connotations, as if there is something wrong with the child or it's her fault that she's having a difficult time with reading. At the 2005 NCTE conference, I had several conversations with teachers about these terms. One person felt *struggling readers* was too connected to a deficit model. Another person suggested reversing how we say it—that *readers who struggle* at least acknowledges them as readers first and strugglers second. But it was Peter Johnston who offered a suggestion that rang true for me. He commented by saying, "Why do we always call them the 'hardest-to-teach' kids when they are actually the 'hardest-for-me-to-teach'?" That made sense to me. We need to take the onus off the struggling reader. It's not his fault. The child certainly doesn't want to be struggling. But he has not been able to learn in the way that we've been teaching him. It is up to us, the teachers, to learn how to teach him better.

So maybe a change in the label is in order. Something more upbeat might keep teachers from feeling weighed down by the load of struggling readers. Perhaps a new name, a more positive label, could begin to change attitudes. Perhaps we should call them:

Inspiring children—because they inspire us to search out more information, improve our teaching, and try new techniques in order to teach them better.

Be all that you can be kids—because their very existence stretches us to be the best teachers we can be at every moment of the school day.

Rewarding readers—because of the rewards we reap when they succeed. It feels so good to have accomplished something with them, to see them take on a strategy and make it their own.

Perhaps some day we'll know struggling readers by a new name—or better yet, perhaps some day there will be no reason to name them at all.

Our Commitment to Children

Koichiro Matsuura, UNESCO's director-general, once said,

> Literacy is inseparable from opportunity, and opportunity is inseparable from freedom. The freedom promised by literacy is both freedom from—from ignorance, oppression, poverty—and freedom to—to do new things, to make choices, to learn.

I love this quote. I keep a copy of it framed on my desk at home. I hung it on the wall in the adult bathrooms of the school I work in. I probably reread it a few times a week. It reminds me of how big our job is and how important we are in the lives of children. We are the ones who teach them to read. It reminds me of our responsibilities to each and every child, not just the ones for whom learning to read comes easily. It speaks to me of how powerful literacy is, powerful enough to change the lives of some children, to lift them out of the cycle of poverty.

As a teacher of reading it's my job to make literacy happen for all the children I come in contact with. I have become an advocate for struggling readers because I believe in their right to become proficient readers and writers just like every other child. We can't pass off the job of teaching the hardest-to-teach children in our rooms to parent volunteers, to teaching assistants, or to a specialist who comes by a few times a week. We have to make the silent promise to all the struggling readers we teach, "Yes, I will teach you to read."

I'd like to leave teachers with a few questions to ponder. Think about yourself, your team, your whole staff, or your school district as you read them.

What will it take for all of us—every teacher of reading—:

- To understand reading process as a network of strategies that each reader constructs for himself?
- To grasp how important explicit modeling and gradual release is for struggling readers?
- To believe that the struggling readers in our school belong to all of us, that we can't pass them off, but need instead to work together to support them?
- To make the most of every teaching encounter with a struggling reader?

The answers you come up with may direct your next learning journey.

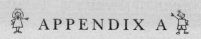

Notes on Listening to a Child Read Orally

(A reflection sheet to determine next steps of instruction)

Child's Name _____ Grade _____ Date _____

Title of Book _____ Level of Text _____

1. What strategies or behaviors do you notice the child using at the point of difficulty?
    Check off each time you notice the child doing one of the following:
    Appeals to you
    Uses pictures
    Sounds the letters
    Rereads
    Reads ahead and returns
    Looks for parts/chunks in unknown word
    Substitutes another word that makes sense
    Skips some words, but meaning isn't changed
    Cross-checks (uses letters as well as meaning and/or structure)
    Self-monitors (notices that something's wrong)
    Self-corrects (fixes the error)

    Reflect: Think about the child's plan for problem solving when reading. Does he rely too much on any one strategy or behavior? What does he need to learn to do to become a better word solver? Write your comments here:

2. List specific errors here. If corrected, add SC.
    Examples: <u>house</u>   <u>mouses</u>   <u>gived/SC</u>
                 home   mice   gave

Reflect: Review each error. Was the child using meaning, structure, visual information, or a combination of those? Did she make multiple attempts? Is there a pattern to the errors? Was she able to SC often?

3. Make a notation concerning the child's pacing, phrasing, expression, and punctuation use.

Reflect: Does he read word by word or in groups of words, like natural talk sounds? Does he "read the punctuation" to make sense of text? Does he use expression to help him make meaning? Does he slow down to problem-solve and then pick up the pace?

4. Comprehension. Have the child retell the book or section that she read aloud. You can use probing questions to get the child to expand or clarify.

Reflect: Was the child able to retell the major points without prompting? Do you feel she understood the main ideas presented in the passage or did she miss the major gist? What did the child do to make you realize she understood (e.g., laughed at a funny part; made a comment; connected to a similar book or experience)?

5. Add any other observations here:

Form developed by Terri Smith and Pat Johnson.

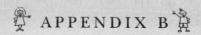

Tess' *At the Zoo* Book

At the zoo By Tess Pardini	 Look. A zebra.
 Look at the tiger.	 Look. The elephant.
 Look at the lion.	 Look out!

Allen, V. 1994. "Selecting Materials for the Reading Instruction of ESL Children." In *Kids Come in All Languages: Reading Instruction for ESL Students,* ed. K. Spangenberg-Urbschat and R. Pritchard. Newark, DE: International Reading Association.

Allington, R. 2000. *What Really Matters for Struggling Readers: Designing Research-Based Programs.* New York: Longman.

———. 2006. "Research and the Three Tier Model." *Reading Today* (April/May): 23 (5): 20.

Allington, R. L., and A. McGill-Franzen. 1995. *No Quick Fix: Rethinking Literacy Programs in America's Elementary Schools.* New York: Teachers College Press.

Anderson, N. 1999. "Language Patterns That May Help or Hinder Learning: Taking an Inventory of Your Assumptions." *Network News* (Spring): 7–11.

Askew, B. J., and I. Fountas. 1996. "Active from the Start." *The Running Record* 9 (1): 1, 6–7, 12–13.

———. 1998. "Building an Early Reading Process: Active from the Start!" *The Reading Teacher* 52 (2): 126–34.

Beers, K. 2003. *When Kids Can't Read: What Teachers Can Do: A Guide for Teachers 6–12.* Portsmouth, NH: Heinemann.

Berk, L. E., and A. Winsler. 1995. *Scaffolding Children's Learning: Vygotsky and Early Childhood Education.* Washington, DC: National Association for the Education of Young Children.

Bomer, R., and K. Bomer. 2001. *For a Better World: Reading and Writing for Social Action.* Portsmouth, NH: Heinemann.

Brand, M. 2004. *Word Savvy: Integrated Vocabulary, Spelling, and Word Study, Grades 3–6.* Portland, ME: Stenhouse.

Cappellini, M. 2005. *Balancing Reading and Language Learning: A Resource for Teaching English Language Learners, K–5.* Portland, ME: Stenhouse.

Clay, M. M. 1987. "Learning to Be Learning Disabled." *New Zealand Journal of Educational Studies* 22: 155–73.

———. 1991. *Becoming Literate: The Construction of Inner Control.* Portsmouth, NH: Heinemann.

———. 1993a. *An Observation Survey of Early Literacy Achievement.* Portsmouth, NH: Heinemann.

———. 1993b. *Reading Recovery: A Guidebook for Teachers in Training.* Portsmouth, NH: Heinemann.

———. 1998. *By Different Paths to Common Outcomes.* Portland, ME: Stenhouse.

———. 2001. *Change over Time in Children's Literacy Development.* Portsmouth, NH: Heinemann.

Collins, K. 2004. *Growing Readers: Units of Study in the Primary Classroom.* Portland, ME: Stenhouse.

Cowley, J. 1988. *The Gumby Shop.* Auckland, New Zealand: Shortland Publications Limited.

Davey, B. 1983. "Thinking Aloud: Modeling the Cognitive Processes of Reading Comprehension." *Journal of Reading* 27: 44–47.

DiCamillo, K. 2000. *Because of Winn-Dixie.* Cambridge, MA: Candlewick Press.

———. 2001. *The Tiger Rising.* Cambridge, MA: Candlewick Press.

Dickens, C. 2004. *A Tale of Two Cities.* New York: Pocket Books.

Dorn, L., C. French, and T. Jones. 1998. *Apprenticeship to Literacy: Transitions Across Reading and Writing.* Portland, ME: Stenhouse.

Dorn, L., and C. Soffos. 2001. *Shaping Literate Minds: Developing Self-Regulated Learners.* Portland, ME: Stenhouse.

Dorris, M. 1999. *The Window.* New York: Hyperion Paperbacks for Children.

Fay, K., and S. Whaley. 2004. *Becoming One Community: Reading and Writing with English Language Learners.* Portland, ME: Stenhouse.

———. 2004/2005. "The Gift of Attention." *Educational Leadership* (December/January): 76–79.

Fielding, L., and P. D. Pearson. 1994. "Reading Comprehension: What Works?" *Educational Leadership* 51 (5): 62–67.

Fletcher, R. 1998. *Flying Solo.* New York: Clarion Books.

Fountas, I. C., and G. S. Pinnell. 1996. *Guided Reading: Good First Teaching for All Children.* Portsmouth, NH: Heinemann.

———. 1998. *Voices on Word Matters: Learning About Phonics and Spelling in the Literacy Classroom.* Portsmouth, NH: Heinemann.

———. 2001. *Guiding Readers and Writers, Grades 3–6.* Portsmouth, NH: Heinemann.

Fox, M. 1992. *Hattie and the Fox.* Cambridge, MA: Candlewick Press.

Garcia, G. 1994. "Assessing the Literacy Development of Second-Language Students: A Focus on Authentic Assessment." In *Kids Come in All Languages: Reading Instruction for ESL Students,* ed. K. Spangenberg-Urbschat and R. Pritchard. Newark, DE: International Reading Association.

Graves, D. H. 1984. "The Enemy Is Orthodoxy." In *A Researcher Learns to Write.* Portsmouth, NH: Heinemann.

———. 2001. *The Energy to Teach.* Portsmouth, NH: Heinemann.

Harvey, S., and A. Goudvis. 2000. *Strategies That Work: Teaching Comprehension to Enhance Understanding.* Portland, ME: Stenhouse.

Hindley, J. 1996. *In the Company of Children.* Portland, ME: Stenhouse.

Hoyt, L. 2002. *Make It Real: Strategies for Success with Informational Texts.* Portsmouth, NH: Heinemann.

Johnston, P. 2000. *Running Records: A Self-Tutoring Guide.* Portland, ME: Stenhouse.

———. 2004. *Choice Words: How Our Language Affects Children's Learning.* Portland, ME: Stenhouse.

Johnston, P., P. Afflerbach, and R. Allington. 1985. "The Congruence of Classroom and Remedial Reading Instruction." *Elementary School Journal* 85: 465.

Keene, E., and S. Zimmerman. 1997. *Mosaic of Thought: Teaching Comprehension in a Reader's Workshop.* Portsmouth, NH: Heinemann.

King-Smith, D. 1983. *Babe: The Gallant Pig.* New York: Alfred A. Knopf.

Leahy, S., C. Lyon, M. Thompson, and D. William. 2005. "Classroom Assessment Minute by Minute, Day by Day." *Educational Leadership* (November): 19–24.

Lipton, L., and B. Wellman. 1998. *Pathways to Understandings: Patterns and Practices in the Learner-Focused Classroom.* Guilford, VT: Pathways.

Lyons, C. 2003. *Teaching Struggling Readers: How to Use Brain-Based Research to Maximize Learning.* Portsmouth, NH: Heinemann.

Lyons, C. A., and G. S. Pinnell. 2001. *Systems for Change in Literacy Education: A Guide to Professional Development.* Portsmouth, NH: Heinemann.

McCarrier, A. 2003. "Teaching for Phrasing and Fluency: Connections to Comprehension." In *Teaching for Comprehension in Reading, Grades K–2.* Gay Su Pinnell and Patricia L. Scharer. New York: Scholastic.

McCarrier, A., G. S. Pinnell., and I. Fountas. 2000. *Interactive Writing: How Language and Literacy Come Together, K–2.* Portsmouth, NH: Heinemann.

McCourt, F. 1996. *Angela's Ashes.* New York: Scribner.

McNaughton, S. 1985. Beyond Teaching. The Development of Independence in Learning to Read. Conference Address. 11th Annual Australian Reading Association. Brisbane.

Melser, J. 1998. *Lazy Mary.* Bothell, WA: The Wright Group.

Melville, H. 1981. *Moby Dick.* New York: Bantam Books.

Mere, C. 2005. *More Than Guided Reading: Finding the Right Instructional Mix, K–3.* Portland, ME: Stenhouse.

Miller, D. 2002. *Reading with Meaning: Teaching Comprehension in the Primary Grades.* Portland, ME: Stenhouse.

Mooney, M. E. 1990. *Reading to, with, and by Children.* Katonah, NY: Richard C. Owen.

Morrison, I. 1994. *Getting It Together: Linking Reading Theory to Practice.* Bothell, WA: The Wright Group.

O'Leary, S. 1997. *Five Kids: Stories of Children Learning to Read.* Bothall, WA: The Wright Group/McGraw Hill.

Parker, E., and Pardini, T. 2006. *"The Words Came Down!" English Language Learners Read, Write, and Talk Across the Curriculum, K–2.* Portland, ME: Stenhouse.

Parkes, B. 2000. *Read It Again! Revisiting Shared Reading.* Portland, ME: Stenhouse.

Payne, C. 2005. *Shared Reading for Today's Classroom.* New York: Scholastic.

Pearson, P. D., and M. C. Gallagher. 1983. "The Instruction of Reading Comprehension." *Contemporary Educational Psychology* 8: 317–344.

Pinnell, G. S., and I. Fountas. 1999. *Word Matters: Teaching Phonics and Spelling in the Reading/Writing Classroom.* Portsmouth, NH: Heinemann.

Pinnell, G. S., and P. Scharer. 2003. *Teaching for Comprehension in Reading, Grades K–2.* New York: Scholastic.

Rathbone, M. 2001. *A Tree Horse.* Barrington, IL: Rigby.

Reading Today. "Meeting Spotlights ELL Issues." *Reading Today.* Newark, DE: International Reading Association.

Robb, L. 1998. *Easy-to-Manage Reading and Writing Conferences: Practical Ideas for Making Conferences Work.* New York: Scholastic.

Rosenblatt, L. [1938] 1983. *Literature as Exploration.* New York: Modern Language Association.

———. 1994. *The Reader, the Text, the Poem: The Transactional Theory of the Literary Work.* Rev. ed. Carbondale, IL: Southern Illinois University Press.

Routman, R. 2003. *Reading Essentials: The Specifics You Need to Teach Reading Well.* Portsmouth, NH: Heinemann.

Rumelhart, D. E. 1994. "Toward an Interactive Model of Reading." In *Theoretical Models and Processes of Reading,* eds. R. B. Ruddell, M. R. Ruddell, and H. Singer. 4th ed. 864–894. Newark, DE: International Reading Association.

Schlein, M. 1992. *The Year of the Panda.* New York: HarperTrophy.

Schulman, M. 2006. *Guided Reading in Grades 3–6: Everything You Need to Make Small-Group Reading Instruction Work in Your Classroom.* New York: Scholastic.

Schulman, M., and C. Payne. 2000. *Guided Reading: Making It Work.* New York: Scholastic.

Schwarz, C. 2000. *Drowning Ruth.* New York: Ballantine Books.

Serafini, F. 2004. *Lessons in Comprehension: Explicit Instruction in the Reading Workshop.* Portsmouth, NH: Heinemann.

Short, K., J. Harste, and C. Burke. 1995. *Creating Classrooms for Authors and Inquirers.* Portsmouth, NH: Heinemann.

Sibberson, F., and K. Szymusiak. 2003. *Still Learning to Read: Teaching Students in Grades 3–6.* Portland, ME: Stenhouse.

Singer, H. 1994. "The Substrata-Factor Theory of Reading." In *Theoretical Models and Processes of Reading,* ed. R. Ruddell and H. Singer. 4th ed. Newark, DE: International Reading Association.

Smith, F. 1994. *Understanding Reading.* Hillsdale, NJ: Lawrence Erlbaum.

———. 1998. *The Book of Learning and Forgetting.* New York: Teachers College Press.

Snowball, D. 2000. *Focus on Spelling.* Videotape. Portland, ME: Stenhouse.

Snowball, D., and F. Bolton. 1999. *Spelling K–8: Planning and Teaching.* Portland, ME: Stenhouse.

Spinelli, J. 1997. *Wringer.* New York: HarperCollins.

Steig, W. 1977. *Caleb and Kate.* New York: Scholastic.

Strickland, D., K. Ganske, and J. Monroe. 2002. *Supporting Struggling Readers and Writers: Strategies for Classroom Intervention 3–6.* Portland, ME: Stenhouse.

Szymusiak, K., and F. Sibberson. 2001. *Beyond Leveled Books: Supporting Transitional Readers in Grades 2–5*. Portland, ME: Stenhouse.

Tharp, R. G., and R. Gallimore. 1988. *Rousing Minds to Life*. New York: Cambridge University Press.

Tovani, C. 2000. *I Read It, but I Don't Get It*. Portland, ME: Stenhouse.

———. 2004. *Do I Really Have to Teach Reading? Content Comprehension, Grades 6–12*. Portland, ME: Stenhouse.

Van Leeuwen, J. 1989. *The Great Cheese Conspiracy*. Boston: Houghton Mifflin.

Vygotsky, L. 1978. *Mind in Society: The Development of Higher Psychological Processes*. Ed. and trans. M. Cole, V. John-Steiner, S. Scribner, and E. Souberman. Cambridge, MA: Harvard University Press.

Waddell, M. 1986. *Owl Babies*. New York: Aladdin Paperbooks.

Wilhelm, J. 2001. *Improving Comprehension with Think Aloud Strategies*. New York: Scholastic.

Wilhelm, J., T. Baker, and J. Dube. 2001. *Strategic Reading: Guiding Students to Lifelong Literacy, 6–12*. Portsmouth, NH: Heinemann.

Wilson, L. 2002. *Reading to Live: How to Teach Reading for Today's World*. Portsmouth, NH: Heinemann.

Wood, D. 1988. *How Children Think and Learn*. Malden, MA: Blackwell.

Wood, D., J. Bruner, and G. Ross. 1976. "The Role of Tutoring in Problem Solving." *Journal of Child Psychology and Problem Solving* 17 (2): 89–100.

accuracy rates, for running
    records, 156, 157, 163
active participation, 27–48
    encouraging, 28, 30, 31, 48
    by English language learners,
        29–35
    "here's what/so what/now
        what/then what framework,
        29–35
    now what stage, 31–33
    scaffolds supporting, 41–43
    setting tone for, 35–36
    so what stage, 31
    teacher role in, 35–36
    then what stage, 34–35
    in word-solving, 6, 28
Allen, V. G., 149
Allington, Richard, 5, 173
Amelia Bedelia books (Parrish),
    141
Anderson, N., 143
Apprenticeship to Literacy (Dorn,
    French, and Jones), 175
appropriate-level texts, 47
Askew, B. J., 28
assessment, 153–70
    acquiring detailed student
        information, 153
    benchmarking, 169
    of English language learners,
        151
    individual reading conferences,
        164–65

ongoing, need for, 154–55
on-the-spot decisions, 168–69
running records, 155–64
tailoring to student needs, 153
three-paneled display board
    for, 176
assessment walls, 176
automatic processing, of strate-
    gies, 46
awkward language structure,
    131–33

Babe: The Gallant Pig (King-
    Smith), 120–21
background knowledge
    activating, in book introduc-
        tions, 129, 130
    English language learners and,
        130
    running records analysis, 159–60
    word-solving using, 37–38
backing off
    defined, 9
    in now what stage, 9
    responsive teaching and, 38, 41
Bailey's Elementary School, 11,
    128, 178
balanced literacy approach, 20–24
    classroom organization and,
        147–49
    for English language learners,
        29
    resources for, 23

Balancing Reading and Language
    Learning: A Resource for
    Teaching English Language
    Learners, K–5 (Cappellini),
    147
basal reading levels, 25
Because of Winn-Dixie (DiCamillo),
    79
Becoming One Community (Fay and
    Whaley), 96, 146
beginning letter use
    explicit demonstrations of,
        32
    introducing, 31–32
    picture symbol scaffold, 41–42
    prompting, 32–33
benchmarking, 169
Big Books, 22, 36, 107–8, 149
    finger pointing with, 67–68
    fluency and, 60
blank books, making, 111
Bokus, Daisy, 101–6
bold print, vocabulary words in,
    65
Bolton, Faye, 107
Bomer, Katherine, 4
Bomer, Randy, 4
book choice
    appropriate-level texts, 47–48
    assistance with, 74, 78
    comprehension and, 74, 76
    for English language learners,
        149–50

192   *One Child at a Time*

book choice (*cont.*)
    finding interesting books,
      60–61
    fluency and, 59–61
    matching students to novels, 94
    for shared reading, 149
book clubs
    monitoring student compre-
      hension in, 74, 79–82
    reading motivation and, 74
    for teachers, 176
book introductions, 45, 51
    background knowledge, 129,
      130
    book title, 129, 130
    Developmental Reading
      Assessment (DRA), 130
    for English language learners,
      58, 129–31
    fluency and, 56–59, 70
    illustrations, 129
    for later-emergent texts, 115
    length of, 130–31
    lengthy sentences, 66–67
    novel punctuation, 66–67
    self-monitoring and, 115
    student connections and, 57,
      59
    summarizing book, 130
    as teaching, 129–30
    vocabulary words for English
      language learners, 137–39
    for voice/print matching, 109
books, student-made
    hidden windows in, 114
    patterns in, 111–14
    self-monitoring and, 111–14
    student names in, 113
books, teacher-made, 108, 109,
    183
Bruner, J., 41
buddy reading, 24, 77
Burke, C., 96
By Different Paths to Common
    Outcomes (Clay), 5, 129

Caleb and Kate (Steig), 89–92
Cappellini, M., 58, 147
challenge books, 47, 74, 76–77
Change Over Time in Children's
    Literacy Development (Clay),
    46
chapter books. *See also* novels
    creating chapter titles for, 81
    guided reading lessons for,
      93–94

matching students to text, 94
reading purpose for chapters,
    94
self-monitoring comprehen-
    sion with, 79–82
value of reading, 93
characters
    charting, 117
    comprehension strategies, 80
    helping students with names
      of, 115
    self-monitoring, 116–17
    speakers tags, 118–20
    tracking dialogue, 117–21
    understanding setting through,
      122–25
Choice Words: How Our Language
    Affects Children's Learning
    (Johnston), 36
choppy reading, 51–56. *See also*
    word-by-word reading
classroom community, 146–47
classroom organization, 147–49
clauses
    at ends of sentences, 64
    separated by commas, 65
Clay, Marie, 4, 5, 15, 17, 18, 20,
    28, 35, 37, 45, 46, 56–57,
    128, 129, 130, 132, 143, 155,
    162–64, 172, 173
coding text, for comprehension,
    78, 96
collaboration, by teachers, 11,
    174–76, 178
commas in a series, 168
communication, with English lan-
    guage learners, 143–46
comprehension, 116, 143–46. *See*
    also reading without compre-
    hension
    anchor lesson on, 75, 85–87
    book choice and, 74, 76–78
    causes of confusion, 165–66
    commas in a series and, 168
    context clues and, 78, 87–92
    defined, 85
    feedback and, 36
    lack of, 75, 85–86, 165–66
    mini-lessons, 85–92, 106–7
    problems testing, 84
    punctuation and, 78, 167–68
    self-monitoring for, 71–98
    stopping when meaning is lost,
      75–76
    student awareness of, 77,
      85–87

student responsibility for moni-
    toring, 83–87
sustained, with novels, 93, 98
teacher activity, 166
teacher monitoring, 81–82, 84
teacher observation, 7, 143–46
visualizing and, 18
comprehension strategies, 17
    character development, 80
    inferring, 80–81
    picking out important parts, 81
    point of view, 81
    responding to text, 81
    self-monitoring setting
      changes, 80
    visualizing, 79–80
comprehension techniques
    coding text, 78–79
    highlighting text, 78
    marking places of confusion,
      79
connections, book introductions
    and, 57, 59
Conques, Kara, 51–56, 121
context, comprehension and,
    87–88
context clues
    charts, 78, 89–91
    for English language learners,
      138–39
    figuring word meanings from,
      87–92
    lesson, 87–92
    on-the-spot assessments and,
      169
controlled vocabulary books, 149
conversations, with English lan-
    guage learners, 143–46
Cowley, Joy, 61
creative arts, 148, 149
cross-checking, 7, 18, 44

dashes, 64–65
Davey, Beth, 96
decodable texts, 149
definitions, recognizing signal
    words for, 65
demonstrations
    beginning letter use, 32
    explicit, 32–33, 36, 167
    reading on, 40–41
    respectful behavior, 146–47
    shared, 36
    strategies, 32–33, 167
determining importance strategy,
    18

developing readers, 24, 25, 156
Developmental Reading
    Assessment (DRA), 169
  book introductions, 130
  leveled texts in, 25
dialogue
  direct address, 64
  mini-lessons, 118–21
  speaker tags and, 64, 118–20
DiCamillo, Kate, 74, 79
dictionaries, 92
direct address, 64
Dorn, Linda, 9, 10, 23, 170, 175,
    176
DRA test levels, 25
Drowning Ruth (Schwarz), 118

easy books, 47, 74, 76–77
*Easy to Manage Reading and
    Writing Conferences* (Robb),
    170
ellipses, 64 65
emergent books, 30
emergent readers, 24, 25
  book selection for, 150
  running records for, 156
  self-monitoring with, 107–16
"Enemy Is Orthodoxy, The"
    (Graves), 42
English language learners
    (ELLs), 127–52
  active participation by, 29–35
  assessment of, 151
  awkward language structures
      and, 131–33
  background knowledge and,
      130
  balanced literacy approach for,
      29
  book introductions for, 58,
      129–31
  book selection for, 149–50
  building classroom community
      for, 146–47
  context clues for, 138–39
  conversations with, 143–46
  figurative language and, 140–41
  illustrations as cues for, 30
  intonation and, 62
  irregular verbs and, 133–34
  language use by, 58–59
  listening to, 143–46
  mnemonic devices for, 134–35
  negotiating meaning with, 145
  number of, 151–52
  observation of, 151

organizing instruction for,
    147–49
out-of-text examples for,
    132–33, 134
present tense use by, 58–59
reading issues for, 131–41
as struggling readers, 127–28
supporting, 143–52
teachers and, 128–31, 143–52
variety in, 127–28
verb tense and, 133–34
visual analogies for, 134
vocabulary issues, 30, 134–40
exclamation points, 62
explicit demonstrations (model-
    ing), 9, 32–33, 36. *See also*
    demonstrations
expressive reading, punctuation
    and, 62–63. *See also* fluency

Fay, Kathleen, 36, 39–40, 79, 127,
    132, 145, 146
feedback, 36
Felderman, Carol, 60–61
Fielding, Linda, 9
figurative language, 140–41
finger pointing
  fluency and, 67–68
  self-monitoring with, 107–8
  voice/print matching and, 109
first letter use. *See* beginning let-
    ter use
flashbacks, self-monitoring, 80
fluency, 49–70
  aspects of, 50
  Big Books and, 60
  book choice and, 59–61
  book introductions and, 56–59,
      70
  elements of, 49–50, 70
  high-frequency word practice
      for, 51
  intonation and, 61–62
  novel language structures and,
      58–59
  observing, 7, 50–51
  practicing, 69
  predicting words and, 56
  punctuation and, 62–67, 70
  reading speed and, 50, 69–70
  rereading and, 51, 70
  self-monitoring for, 55–56, 70
  shared reading and, 60
  strategies for, 51–56
  thinking aloud about, 68–69
  word-solving and, 50, 56

fluent readers, 24, 25. *See also* pro-
    ficient readers
  individualized reading confer-
      ences for, 156–57
Flying Solo (Fletcher), 117
Fountas, Irene C., 9, 17, 18, 20,
    23, 24, 28, 107, 155
Fountas and Pinnell leveled texts,
    25
Fox, Mem, 60
framework, 5–11
framing groups of words, 52–53
French, Cathy, 23, 175
Frey, Jean, 11

Gallagher, T., 9
Gallimore, R., 10, 42, 96
Ganske, K., 69
Garcia, G., 151
Garfield Elementary School, 128
gender words, English language
    learners and, 146
"Gift of Attention, The" (Fay and
    Whaley), 145
Goudvis, Anne, 20, 79, 95, 97
gradual release of responsibility,
    9, 167
Graves, Donald, 42, 175–76
Great Cheese Conspiracy, The (Van
    Leeuwen), 122–26
guided reading
  introducing lengthy sentences,
      66–67
  practicing strategies in, 45–46
  purpose of, 23
  through a novel, 93–94
*Guided Reading: Good First Teaching
    for All Children* (Fountas and
    Pinnell), 155
Guided Reading: Making It Work
    (Schulman and Payne), 24,
    155, 170
Gumby Shop, The (Cowley), 61

"hardest-to-teach children,"
    178–79
Harste, J., 96
Harvey, Stephanie, 20, 79, 95, 97
Henry and Mudge books
    (Rylant), 168
"here's what/so what/now what/
    then what" framework
  active participation, 29–35
  collaborative use of, 178
  defined, 5
  fluency, 50–56

"here's what/so what/now what/
    then what" framework *(cont.)*
    foundations for, 13–14
    steps in, 5–11
    using with teachers, 11
here's what stage
    active participation, 29–30
    assessment and, 154
    description, 5–7
    English language learners and,
        151
    fluency, 50–51
    importance of, 18–19
    self-monitoring, 72–73, 100–101
    teacher observation methods, 7
hidden windows, in student-made
    books, 114
high-frequency words
    activities with, 108
    practicing, for fluency, 51
highlighting text, for comprehen-
    sion, 78, 95–96
Hindley, J., 170

idioms, 140–41, 142
illustrations
    as cues for English language
        learners, 30
    discussing in book introduc-
        tions, 129
    picture symbol scaffold, 41–42
    searching, running records
        analysis of, 159
importance, determining, 18, 81
independent readers, 24, 25,
    156–57
independent reading strategies,
    45–46
individual reading
    classroom organization for,
        147–48
    purpose of, 23–24
    rereading books in, 61
individual reading conferences,
    164–65
    information provided by, 154
    note-taking form, 165, 181–82
    running records *vs.,* 156–57
inferring, 79–81
inflection, fluency and, 50
inner thought, 45
interactive read-alouds, 22
In the Company of Children
    (Hindley), 170
intonation
    English language learners and, 62

fluency and, 61–62
I Read It, but I Don't Get It
    (Tovani), 85
irregular verbs, English language
    learners and, 133–35

Johnston, Peter, 36, 155, 157,
    178–79
Jones, Tammy, 23, 175
just right books, 47, 74, 76

Keene, Ellin, 17, 20, 84
Keier, Katie, 128–31, 133–34
Kennedy, John F., 50
*Kids Come in All Languages:
    Reading Instruction for ESL
    Students* (Allen), 149
King, Martin Luther, Jr., 50
King-Smith, Dick, 120
Kurtz, Nancy, 39–40
KWL charts, 95

labeling, 36, 178–79
Language Arts, 178
language use
    by English language learners,
        58–59
    practicing awkward structures,
        132–33
    preparing students for unusual
        structure, 115, 131–33
    by teachers, 36
later-emergent texts, 114–15
Lazy Mary (Melser), 60
Leahy, S., 154
learning how to learn, 35
lengthy sentences, preparing stu-
    dents for, 66–67
letters, searching, 159
letter sounds, 103–5
leveled texts, 24, 25
Lipton, Laura, 5
listening
    to English language learners,
        143–46
    respect and, 147
literacy
    balanced literacy approach,
        20–22, 23, 29
    power of, 179–80
literacy club, 36
Literacy Collaborative (LC), 177
literacy environment, 20–24
Literacy Learning Groups (LLG),
    177
literary-processing theory, 172

looping marks, in running
    records, 55
Lowe, Stanzi, 68–69, 134
Lyons, C. A., 45, 93, 96, 175

Maher, Jodi, 60
Matsuura, Koichiro, 179
McCarrier, Andrea, 67–68
McCourt, Frank, 87, 121
McDonnell, Laura, 29–35
McGill-Franzen, A., 5
meaning
    construction of, 75
    intonation and, 61–62
    stopping when meaning is lost,
        75–76
    word-solving using, 6, 14–16,
        33, 34, 37, 51, 56, 161–62
memorizing language structures,
    132–33
Mere, Cathy, 23, 164
Miller, Debbie, 9, 95
mini-lessons
    dialogue, 118–21
    dividing over several days, 92
    length of, 92
    monitoring for understanding,
        85–87
    resources for, 106–7
mnemonic devices, 134–35
modeling. *See also* demonstrations
    active participation, 36
    comprehension strategies, 167
    defined, 8
    in now what stage, 8–9
    responsive teaching and, 38
monotone reading, 50
Monroe, J., 69
Mooney, M. E., 20
More Than Guided Reading (Mere),
    164
Morrison, I., 157
Mosaic of Thought (Keene and
    Zimmerman), 84
motivation for reading, 73, 74,
    82, 115

names
    using in student books, 113
    voice/print matching activities
        with, 108
Naylor, Noel, 35
network of strategies, 13–14,
    17–20, 35, 43, 95, 126, 154.
    See also strategies
Newsweek, 116–17

nonfiction
  appeal to struggling readers,
    93
  vocabulary words in, 65
nonsense words, self-monitoring,
    101–2
note-taking
  form for, 165, 181–82
  in individual reading confer-
    ences, 165
  on student strategy use, 10
novel language structures, 58–59
novel punctuation use, 66–67
novels. *See also* chapter books
  guided reading lessons for,
    93–94
  guiding struggling readers,
    93–94
  matching students to text, 94
  reading purpose for chapters,
    94
  sustained comprehension with,
    93, 98
now what stage
  active participation, 31–33
  assessment and, 154
  fluency, 52–55
  self-monitoring, 74–82, 102–5
  teacher actions for, 8–10

observation
  of comprehension, 143–46
  of English language learners,
    151
  of fluency issues, 7, 50–51
  in here's what stage, 6–7
  of predicting words, 6
  of self-monitoring, 73, 82–83
  of struggling readers, 2, 13
  of student efforts to fix com-
    prehension, 7
  of student use of strategies,
    6–11, 20, 43–44, 55–56,
    157–62
  of word-by-word reading, 50–51
*Observation Survey of Early Literacy
  Achievement* (Clay), 155
O'Leary, S., 127
Omps, Carrie, 66
out-of-text examples, 132–33
Owl Babies (Waddell), 148

paraphrasing, 79
Pardini, Tess, 108, 147, 183
parent volunteers, 111
Parker, Emelie, 108, 146, 147

Parrish, Peggy, 141
passive readers, 6
  running records for, 30
  teacher behavior and, 31
  text-level, 28
  word-level, 28
*Pathways to Understandings:
  Patterns and Practices in the
  Learner-Focused Classroom*
  (Lipton and Wellman), 5
patterned books
  for English language learners,
    150
  making, 111–14, 150
patterned sentences, 79, 96
patterns, in running records, 157,
    158
Payne, Carleen, 17, 20, 23, 24, 60,
    155, 170
Pearson, P. D., 9
phrases, at ends of sentences, 64
phrasing
  fluency and, 50
  framing words, 52–54
  reading alternate pages, 54
  running records on, 55–56
  self-monitoring, 53–54, 55–56
  sentence strip, 54
  strategies for, 51–56
picture books, reenactments, 148
picture symbol scaffolds, 41–42
Pinnell, Gay Su, 9, 17, 18, 20, 23,
    24, 107, 155, 175
point of view, 81
Powell, Ruth, 173
Powers, Elizabeth, 84
practicing
  awkward language structures,
    132–33
  for fluency, 51, 69
  strategies, 44–46, 48
predicting words
  confirming, 18
  fluency and, 56
  observing, 6
  running records analysis of,
    158
  using meaning, 6
predictions
  about setting, 123–24
  comprehension and, 80
pretending to read, 47
prior knowledge. *See* background
    knowledge
problem-solving strategies, 27–28
professional development, 176–78

proficient readers. *See also* fluent
    readers
  characteristics of, 27–28
  flexible use of strategies by, 28
  fluency of, 28
  networks of strategies used by,
    16–20
  problem-solving strategies of,
    27–28
  reading pace, 70
progressing readers, 24, 25, 156
prompting
  beginning letter use, 32–33
  defined, 8
  inner thought and, 45
  in now what stage, 8–9, 32–33
  picture symbol scaffolds, 41–42
  responsive teaching and, 38
  by tapping table, 41
  for word part sounds, 104
pronoun referents, 169
punctuation
  about fluency, 68–69
  added clauses, 64
  clauses separated by commas,
    65
  comprehension and, 78,
    167–68
  dashes, 64–65
  direct address, 64
  ellipses, 64–65
  explicit teaching of, 63
  expressive reading and, 62–63
  fluency and, 50, 62–67, 70
  modeling in shared reading,
    62–63
  novel, introducing, 66–67
  running records analysis of, 160
  speaker tags before dialogue,
    64
  thinking aloud about, 69

question marks, 62
quotation marks
  absence of, 121
  introducing, 62
  tracking dialogue with, 119

reading
  complex theories of, 172–74
  motivation for, 73, 74, 82, 115
  simple theory of, 171–173
  by teachers, 176
  theories of, 172–74, 177
  vocabulary development dur-
    ing, 46

reading aloud
  classroom organization for, 148
  interactive, 22
  modeling strategies for, 22
  purpose of, 22
  self-monitoring in, 82–83
reading conferences. *See* individual reading conferences
Reading Essentials (Routman), 170
reading on
  demonstrating, 40–41
  for meaning, 40–41
  running records analysis of, 159
reading process, 3–5, 11, 13–14, 16, 28, 31, 43, 48, 95, 96, 153, 155, 162, 164, 170, 172, 173, 180
  chart of reading process, 17
  reading a running record for, 158–162
  and staff development, 172, 175–178
reading programs, 20
Reading Recovery, 25, 35–36, 157, 177
reading speed, 50, 69–70
reading without comprehension. *See also* comprehension
  allowing time for changes, 75, 171–72
  causes of, 116, 166
  limitations of, 71–72, 106
  nonsense words, 101–2
  by passive readers, 28
  running records analysis of, 160–61
  self-monitoring and, 72, 75–83
  student awareness of, 77, 85–87
  taking action, 85–87
  text-level, 28
  word-level, 28
reenactments, of picture books, 148
reinforcing
  defined, 9
  evaluating, 36
  in now what stage, 9, 33
  reading on, 41
  responsive teaching and, 38
repetition, 150
rereading
  benefits of, 45
  finding books children will reread, 60–61
  for fluency, 51, 70

for meaning, 39–40
picture symbol scaffold, 41–42
purposes of, 39
running records analysis of, 159, 160
teaching, 39–40
without thinking, 39–40
respect, for students, 146–47
responding to text
  comprehension strategies, 81
  T-charts for, 81
responsibility
  gradual release of, 9, 167
  for self-monitoring, 83–87
responsive teaching, 8–9, 38
Robb, L., 170
Rosenblatt, Louise, 74
Ross, B., 41
round-robin reading, 71–72
Rousing Minds to Life (Tharp and Gallimore), 10
Routman, Regie, 1, 2, 9, 23, 94, 170
Rumelhart, D. E., 15
running records
  accuracy rates, 156, 157
  analysis of, 157–62
  defined, 155
  information provided by, 154
  looping marks for phrasing, 55
  multiple attempts at word-solving, 44
  for passive readers, 30
  patterns in, 157, 158
  phrasing and, 55–56
  predicting strategies and, 158
  punctuation and, 160
  purposes, 155–56
  searching and gathering strategies and, 159–60
  self-correction (SC) rates, 156, 157
  self-monitoring and, 101, 106, 160–61
  student strategy use and, 10, 45–46, 159–62
  teacher training on, 164
  teaching points and, 156, 157
  using, 156–57
Running Records: A Self-Tutoring Guide (Johnston), 155

"say something" technique, 96
scaffolding
  in now what stage, 8–9
  picture symbols for, 41–42

purpose of, 8, 48
responsive teaching and, 38
supporting active participation with, 41–43
temporary nature of, 42
Scharer, Patricia, 20
Schulman, Mary, 17, 20, 23, 24, 155, 170
Schwarz, Christina, 118
searching and gathering strategies, 159–60
self-congratulations, 163–64
self-correction (SC)
  noting in individual reading conferences, 165
  running records, analysis of, 156, 157, 160, 162–64
self-instruction, 163
self-monitoring, 18
  characters, 116–17
  for comprehension, 71–98
  defined, 6
  dialogue, 117–21
  with emergent readers, 107–16
  fluency and, 55–56, 70
  "here's what/so what/now what/then what" framework, 72–83, 100–106
  lack of, 72, 74, 160–61
  making books for, 111–14
  mini-lessons, 85–92, 106–7
  multiple, 99–126
  observing, 73, 82–83
  for phrasing, 53–54, 55–56
  reading aloud, 82–83
  running records, 101, 160–61
  setting changes, 80, 121–26
  stopping when meaning is lost, 75–76
  student pride in, 83
  student responsibility for, 83–87
  types of, 99–100
  in upper-elementary grades, 116–17
  vocabulary, 87–92
  voice/print match, 107–11
sentences
  lengthy, introducing, 66–67
  patterns, 114
sentence strips, 54
setting
  author hints for, 122
  discussing with partners, 124
  predictions about, 123–24
  self-monitoring changes in, 80, 121–26

Shaping Literate Minds (Dorn and Soffos), 170, 176
shared demonstrations, 36
shared reading, 36
    classroom organization for, 148
    fluency and, 60
    modeling picture symbol scaffolds in, 41
    modeling punctuation marks in, 62–63
    purpose of, 22–23
Shared Reading for Today's Classroom (Payne), 60
Shea, Sabrina, 57
Short, K., 96
Sibberson, F., 83, 117, 166
signal words, for vocabulary definitions, 65
Singer, H., 46
small-group lessons
    assessment in, 167
    classroom organization for, 147–48
Smith, Frank, 36
Snowball, Diane, 107
Soffos, Carla, 9, 10, 176
sounding out
    breaking words apart, 103–5
    overuse of, 37
sources of information
    balancing, 15–16, 161–62
    books on, 17
    for word solving, 14–16
so what stage
    active participation, 31
    assessment and, 154
    description, 7–8
    fluency, 51–52
    self-monitoring, 73–74, 101–2
speaker tags, 64, 118–20
Spelling K–8: Planning and Teaching (Snowball and Bolton), 107
Spinelli, Jerry, 68–69
staff development, 176–78
standardized reading tests, 71
Steig, William, 89, 92
sticky notes, making hidden windows with, 114
Still Learning to Read: Teaching Students in Grades 3–6 (Sibberson and Szymusiak), 117
story line, word-solving using, 89
strategies
    active use of, 33, 39–41

allowing time for teaching, 75, 98, 171–72
    automatic use of, 34, 46
    balancing use of, 15–16, 38–39, 48
    defined, 95
    effectiveness of, 97
    explicit demonstration of, 32–33
    flexible, 27–29
    for fluency, 51–56
    in guided reading, 45–46
    in independent reading, 45–46
    initial processing of, 46
    learning, 34–35
    multiple attempts, 135–37, 162, 172
    network of, 16–20, 19–20, 35, 43, 95, 126, 154
    observing student use of, 8–11, 20, 43–44, 157–62
    picture symbol scaffolds, 41–42
    practicing, 44–46, 48
    of proficient readers, 6–7
    proficient use of, 27–29
    prompting, 32–33
    reinforcing, 33, 41
    resources for, 20
    running records analysis of, 157–62
    simplifying child's role in, 42
    teaching to students, 8–10
    techniques *vs.*, 95, 97
    understanding student use of, 4
Strategies That Work (Harvey and Goudvis), 97
Strickland, D., 69
structural information, for word-solving, 14–16, 37, 161–62
struggling readers, 171
    allowing time for teaching, 75, 98, 171–72
    assessment of, 153–70
    backing off supports to, 2
    balancing information sources, 15, 38–39
    characteristics of, 3–5
    English language learners as, 127–28
    framework for teaching, 5–11
    observing individual difficulties of, 2, 13
    as percentage of all children, 128
    stages of, 24, 25

teacher learning about, 174–76
    teacher support for, 1–2, 3, 173
    teaching strategies to, 2
    terminology, 178–79
summarizing books, 130
sustaining reading strategies, 17
symbols, picture scaffolds, 41–42
Szymusiak, Karen, 83, 117, 166

tapping, to prompt strategy use, 41
T-charts, 81
teachers
    backing off support, 9, 38, 41
    collaboration by, 11, 174–76, 178
    commitment to children by, 179–80
    "here's what/so what/now what/then what" framework and, 11
    knowledge of reading process, 3
    language used by, 36
    learning by, 174–76
    as readers, 176
    support for English language learners, 128–31, 143–52
    support for struggling readers, 1–2, 3, 173
teacher training
    on running records, 164
    staff development, 176–78
    on teaching English language learners, 152
teaching
    "future oriented," 32
    making every moment count, 1–2
Teaching for Comprehension in Reading (Pinnell and Scharer), 67–68
teaching points, for running records, 156, 157
Teaching Struggling Readers (Lyons), 93
techniques, 94–97
    coding text, 78, 96
    defined, 95
    graphic organizers, 95
    highlighting text, 78, 95–96
    KWL charts, 95
    patterned sentences, 79, 96
    "say something" technique, 96
    strategies *vs.*, 95, 97
text gradient systems, 24, 25

Tharp, R. G., 10, 42, 96
then what stage
    active participation, 34–35
    assessment and, 154
    English language learners and, 151
    fluency, 55–56
    observing child's use of strategy in, 10–11
    self-monitoring, 82–83, 105–6
thinking abilities, 172
thinking about story, 41–42
thinking aloud, 68–69
Thompson, Judy, 2
Tiger Rising, The (DiCamillo), 74, 79, 140
titles
    creating, for chapters, 81
    discussing in book introductions, 129, 130
Tovani, Cris, 75, 78, 85, 95, 166
transitional readers, 24, 25, 156
Tree Horse, A (Rathbone), 57

unknown words. *See also* vocabulary; word-solving
    English language learners and, 140
    stopping for, 75–76
upper-elementary grades, self-monitoring in, 116–17

Vander Zanden, Sarah, 73–83, 85, 86
Van Leeuwen, Jean, 122
verb tenses, 133–35
visual analogies, 134
visual information
    running records analysis of, 161
    for word-solving, 14–16, 37, 106, 161–62
visualizing
    comprehension and, 18, 79–80
    self-monitoring dialogue, 121
vocabulary
    context clues, 78, 87–92, 138–39
    English language learners and, 30, 134–40

figurative language, 140–41
learning while reading, 46
nonsense words, 101–2
recognizing definitions in text, 65
self-monitoring, 87–92
unknown words and concepts, 140
words with multiple meanings, 135–37
voice/print matching
    book introductions and, 109
    self-monitoring for, 107–11
    supporting, 109–10
vowel sounds, 105
Vygotsky, Lev, 93, 96

Waddell, Martin, 148
Wednesday workshops, 178
Wellman, Bruce, 5
Whaley, Suzanne, 79, 127, 145, 146
whiteboards
    breaking words apart on, 103–5, 126
    for mnemonic devices, 134–35
whole-class lessons
    assessment of individual students in, 167–68
    classroom organization for, 147–48
Wilhelm, Jeffrey, 9, 95
Wood, D., 41
word-by-word reading
    fluency and, 50
    observing, 50–51
    observing strategy use, 55–56
    providing strategies for, 52–55
    sharing ideas on, 51–52
word cards, for practicing high-frequency words, 51
Word Matters: Teaching Phonics and Spelling in the Reading/Writing Classroom (Pinnell and Fountas), 107
words. *See also* vocabulary; word-solving
    blending together, 108
    with multiple meanings, 135–37

Word Savvy: Integrated Vocabulary, Spelling, and Word Study, Grades 3–6 (Brand), 107
"Words Came Down!, The": English Language Learners Read, Write, and Talk Across the Curriculum, K–2 (Parker and Pardini), 108, 147
word-solving
    active participation in, 6, 27–29
    background knowledge for, 37–38
    balancing cues for, 15–16, 38–39, 48
    beginning letter, 31–33
    breaking words apart, 103–5, 126
    context clues for, 78, 87–92
    cross-checking, 7
    dictionaries and, 92
    flexibility in, 6
    fluency and, 50, 56
    irregular verbs, 134
    meaning and, 37, 51, 56
    multiple attempts at, 43–44, 162
    observing student strategies for, 6–7
    passive, 6
    predicting words using meaning, 6, 33, 34
    searching for information, 6
    sources of information for, 14–16
    story line and, 89
    strategies, 17
    structural information for, 37
    visual information for, 14–16, 37, 106
    words with multiple meanings, 135–37
Wringer (Spinelli), 68–69
writing process, 42

Zimmerman, S., 17, 20, 84
zone of proximal development, 93